Bill Pope

SHARON ORECK
VIDEO SLUT

Sharon Oreck is a film, video, and commercial producer. Between 1986 and 2000 she was the owner-operator of O Pictures. She is an Academy Award nominee and the recipient of a Grammy Award, two Women in Film Awards, and several MTV awards. She lives in Los Angeles.

VIDEO SLUT

VIDEO SLUT

How I Shoved Madonna off an Olympic High Dive,

Got Prince into a Pair of Tiny Purple Woolen Underpants,

Ran Away from Michael Jackson's Dad,

and Got a Waterfall to Flow Backward So I Could Bring

Rock Videos to the Masses

SHARON ORECK

FABER AND FABER, INC.
An affiliate of Farrar, Straus and Giroux   New York

FABER AND FABER, INC.

An affiliate of Farrar, Straus and Giroux

18 West 18th Street, New York 10011

Distributed in Canada by D&M Publishers, Inc.

Printed in the United States of America

First edition, 2010

Library of Congress Cataloging-in-Publication Data

Oreck, Sharon.

Video slut : how I shoved Madonna off an Olympic high dive, got Prince
into a pair of tiny purple woolen underpants, ran away from Michael Jackson's
dad, and got a waterfall to flow backward so I could bring rock videos to the
masses / Sharon Oreck.

p.   cm.

ISBN 978-0-86547-986-9 (pbk. : alk. paper)

1. Oreck, Sharon.   2. Motion picture producers and directors—United
States—Biography.   3. Music videos—Production and direction.   I. Title.

PN1998.3.O74A3 2010

791.4302'32092—dc22

[B]

2009043062

Designed by Abby Kagan

www.fsgbooks.com

1   3   5   7   9   10   8   6   4   2

This is a true story, but some names have been changed to protect privacy.

To Bill, Savannah, Tina,
Harper, Tess, and William
for being the loves of my life.
But even more to
Josh,
who saved me.

Contents

VIDEO SLUT

Sun Comes Up

It's December 12, 1988, and I'm just finishing up lunch with an egregiously hairy, three-hundred-and-forty-pound Geffen Record Company executive who's swaddled in an immaculate knee-length white silk Indian kurta that turns out to be a precise color match for the pearl-handled revolver that he whips out of his size ninety-nine dhoti pantaloons while we're waiting for the parking valet to roll up with his Rolls-Royce Silver Cloud.

"*Et voilà!*" Rod Stovington snorts through his two-inch plank of Santa-Christ facial hair, which is currently flecked with spit, tomato skin, and tiny bits of lacto-vegetarian nut loaf. "I always carry a .357 Magnum, just in case Axl Rose stops taking his lithium and tries to, like, fuckin' impale me with a machete again."

Since he has immediate access to a loaded handgun and has recently awarded me two rock video contracts worth a quarter of a million dollars, I elect not to mention that Rod looks like a deranged three-thousand-year-old Norse deity after a six-week crack binge before I jump into my battered, bird shit–encrusted forest-and-black Saab convertible and wave bye-bye. Then I roll approximately 2,050 feet to the threshold of O Pictures, my hip, happening, totally eighties rock video and commercial production boutique, conveniently located at the ugliest, most architecturally incoherent end of East Melrose Avenue, between Paramount motion picture studios and the Hollywood Theatrical Car Painting Center.

"I'm lucky I was too terrified to eat my truffled risotto at lunch today, because now I'm still thin enough (if I only drink watermelon juice for the next three days) to wear that size-four, lime green, fancy French mermaid dress that I just bought to wear to Madonna's surprise party this weekend for famous movie star Warren Beatty at her recently redecorated, super-sophisticated, white-on-white Bel Air pied à terre!" I muse to myself. "I'm also super lucky that I bought my $800 outfit with a postdated company check because it'll bounce like a lowrider on Saturday night if anyone tries to cash it before next February!"

Although I own a (purportedly) successful, top-tier, totally professional rock video and commercial company that takes in (a rumored) $20 million a year, I am actually poised at the gaping abyss of bankruptcy and shame, due to questionable insurance claims, catastrophic production overages, and the kind of insanely outsize workers' compensation suits that are always being filed by the kind of overly litigious methamphetamine addicts who we always hire to be rock video extras because they're the only kind of people who'll take $50 for a seventeen-hour workday.

Since I'm a (ridiculously) optimistic kind of person, I joyously ram my nonluxury vehicle into my undersized parking space and strut with (false) pride and (faked) confidence toward my (utterly bitchin') silk-screened double doors just as they fling open to disgorge a large, scary clutch of disgruntled twenty-five-year-old women who all happen to be sporting suspiciously similar faux-platinum hair bobs and chocolate-brown Sophia Loren fuck-me slips.

"Well hello, adorable and athletic fake-Madonna stunt double applicants!" I recognize them immediately. "Thanks so much for what I'm sure were your amazing auditions, which I unfortunately missed, due to an important preexisting appointment with a renowned recording industry sociopath! I hope your experience at my company was pleasurable all the same!"

The stunt doubles glare at me with an unsettling degree of aggression before they stomp off into the smog, like bleached-blonde lady Spartans exiting a successful peace conference.

"Not. Fucking. Amazing." Their spokesperson barks at me while attempting to trap my head in the door. Although stunt doubles are psychologically sensitive, like actors, they're physically insensitive, like athletes, with a strong desire to slam you into a wall and fuck you exactly where you never wanted to be fucked just because your company declined to hire them.

I run away, fast, up the new fake-marble stairwell that leads into the old brick-and-stucco photographer's studio that used to look like a decaying New York slum right before we borrowed fifty thousand bucks to make it look like a peeling Caribbean tenement instead. The complex, love/hate affair with money and privilege that defines the late 1980s has led my company to a bold, pseudopoverty design statement that unequivocally declares that we're living in a shit-hole because we can *afford* to live in a shit-hole and not because we *have* to live in a shit-hole.

"Jeepers!" I scream with joy as I hit the second floor landing and unexpectedly encounter a teeming mass of tall, well-built young black men, suggestively garbed in the scanty, tattered robes of ancient Christian martyrs. I guess there is a God after all, and it's not the one my fathers shed their foreskins for.

Then I remember that today is casting day for the "Like a Prayer" video and that what appear to be hunky holy men are actually handsome Hollywood hopefuls who are preparing to vie for the role of Super-Studly African American Iconographic Saint 'n' Super-Vixen who will get to simulate sex with Madonna on a down-at-the-heels church altar in order to end national racism, encourage world peace, and promote the ultimate salvation of the universe until the end of time.

"Welcome to O Pictures, handsome gentlemen!" I greet the dude-a-ciples. Hey, maybe this will turn out to be a nice day after all!

"Hi, lady producer!" They greet me back, patting me fondly as I make my way toward my office. "Love your place! What a great set up! Nice digs!"

"Oh gosh, thank you," I reply. "You are so, so sweet!"

While I am utterly convinced that anyone who hates O Pictures is a lying, scabby child molester, I always believe it when anyone says they love O Pictures, even if they're obviously just trying to butter me up so they can get hired to have rock-video sex for money with a molten-hot pop-music superstar.

"I want O Pictures to offer a colorful, larger-than-life, joy-filled artistic refuge, with a street-ish, fun-factory kind of gestalt," I remember telling my savvy team of (purportedly) homosexual decorators without the slightest edge of irony, which might help to explain the green-and-gold fake-marble reception area that prominently features a gilded three-thousand-pound fax machine, a giant, gold-embossed prop clock from an old Boz Scaggs video, and my steadfast and good-looking male receptionist, Fred Rick, who really is practically perfect if you don't count the constant bids for attention, the steroid abuse leading to occasional temper tantrums and the grotesque temporary speech impediment due to improperly sterilized tongue-piercing equipment.

"Og Biditchas!" (O Pictures). Fred is answering the phone while madly blowing me kisses. "Ow cran I whelp du?"

I wave to Fred gaily, because he is so, well, gay, and continue striding into the yellow-and-blue fake-marble bullpen, a huge, loftlike space where all the full-time workers and all the freelance workers and all those adorable, absolutely-for-free film interns perform the valuable preproduction labor that's necessary to create a successful rock video. Yes, this is where the magic happens, and it's currently happening at full freak-out capacity, on account of a Madonna video, a Metallica video, a Tracy Chapman video, and a commercial for a smelly, disgusting German zit soap.

"Hey boss!"

"Looking good!"

"Awesome outfit!"

"Did you cut your hair?"

"Did you get a facial?"

"Love your boots!"

My company is always packed with fluffy dogs and unwashed children and groovily attired, perfectly coiffed hipster chicks who are always telling me how cool I am and how great I look. Also uniformly present is a scattered handful of sycophantic, sexually ambiguous young gentlemen who sit at long, Formica-covered tabletops, making phone calls, working on gigantic Macintosh computers, and furiously jotting away on yellow legal pads. Because, in many ways, O Pictures is exactly like Paradise Island, the mythical Amazonian home of Wonder Woman and her foxy superheroine sisters, who all live in a bucolic feminist utopia with their obedient man-slaves in perfect harmony—except that O Pictures isn't an island, some of the men are women, and the slaves don't do anything I tell them.

"Guttenfuckenzee! You've got to be joking me out!"

The glamorous blonde lesbian with the cool haircut who is screaming inexplicable phrases in an unidentifiable accent is the (real) executive producer of O Pictures, Hildy Inigborgasson. It's her job to monitor all of our productions, mentor all the line producers, make sure that nobody goes overbudget, and tell all my directors how smart and cute they are, especially when they're stupid and ugly.

Just kidding. As the owner and (not real) executive producer of O Pictures, it's *my* job to remind the directors that they're intelligent and successful, especially when they wet their pants like big, fat babies because their lives are so hard and they have to work thirty days a year so they can afford a top-of-the-line shiny new convertible so they can finally get with some real models, and not just those stupid video extras again.

Once again, I am obviously just kidding. Everyone knows that rock video directors always try to fuck the extras, because they hardly ever press charges.

Meanwhile, next to Hildy is Diana, a striking, twenty-five-year-old woman who's securing the Fort MacArthur Air Force Base as a location for the Madonna "Like a Prayer" video.

"I will not tolerate this reeking bullshit for one second longer, do you hear me?" Diana is saying.

My heart sings! Diana has been here for only eight weeks and she has already evolved into exactly the kind of competent, hard-driving hottie bitch that O Pictures is famous for. At our company, brutal management is to great production what wire foundation is to surgically unaltered bosoms.

Next to Diana is Veronica, who's dressed to kill in a second-hand early-sixties, navy blue Dior suit jacket with pearls.

"Excuse me," Veronica is saying, "but we need to have a remote, soundproof setting where we can turn the volume way, way up, because the band is so completely deaf that they couldn't hear a Concorde jet if it was landing between their legs."

Veronica, who's the most fashionable, good-looking, naturally skinny person I've ever met, is attempting to find an appropriate location for "One," the very first music video from the platinum-selling thrash band Metallica, which my brand-new husband, Bill Pope, is going to direct. My good pal Robin Sloane, who's in charge of creative affairs at Elektra Records, says that Metallica is different from other super-successful thrash bands because they're "brilliant iconoclasts who're way too cool to make a video," but Rod, the psycho Geffen A&R Dude with the gun that I just had lunch with, claims that they're more like "homicidal, alcoholic shit-birds who've been too drunk every minute of the day and night since the late seventies to get anything done." To be fair,

Robin is a genius and the Geffen Executive has been in a drug-induced stupor since 1969 and doesn't actually work with Metallica. Still, the relationship of the band to alcoholic beverages is so mythical that Veronica has written on the budget in huge letters: "FINAL BUDGET DOES NOT INCLUDE BEER."

Next to Veronica is Hunter, Hildy's heartachingly young assistant, who has buttermilk skin and bright blue eyes and a mind-boggling physique that make certain bosses wonder if certain lesbian executives would ever hire a beautiful person just for her buttocks. On the other hand, as the daughter of a famous rock star and his famous model wife, Hunter has an unusual pedigree for meeting unreasonable demands of overentitled celebrity brats.

". . . I hear what you're saying about 'the President' and 'forever,' but I need a system that's guaranteed to keep at least two dozen crosses burning for a week!" Hunter is shouting at the chief caretaker of the JFK Eternal Flame at Arlington National Cemetery. "I mean this is a major, major Madonna video!"

Kennedy, Schmennedy. We've recently experienced some ugly glitches with an underground gas line that might have been illegally dug on an American military base for the "Like a Prayer" video and it's Hunter's job to keep the fires burning, literally. Slated for production early next month with my rock video best-director-friend-forever, Mary Lambert, at the helm, "Like a Prayer" is the biggest, most badass video production of my whole life. On the other hand, it's also the biggest, most badass nightmare of my whole life. The script is endless, the budget is a ball-breaker, and I get twenty threatening phone calls per day from Eddie Grimstein, the head of Creative Affairs at Warner Records, who has been personally determined to crush my soul, spirit, and spinal column ever since Madonna told him in front of me to "shut up, fuck off, and get out the room so the girls can get some real work done."

Here's a free career tip: when a rich and extremely powerful female sex goddess symbolically crushes the (metaphorical) testicles of an extremely powerful man who can in any way affect your future, it is very important that you *do not* in any way acknowledge, approve, or applaud that action *until* he is out of the room, way down the hall, and, hopefully, driving home on the Santa Monica Freeway.

Moving on to the next desk, we find Joy and Lauren, who are putting together a reshoot for Matt Mahurin's latest John Fogerty clip after an official MTV video rejection caused by a semierect penis that was wrapped in five layers of plaster, mud, and medical gauze.

I can still remember Jeff Ayeroff, former vice president of Warner Records, yelling at me over a satellite phone that—because of early-eighties technology—was still the size of a Montana moose, just because I called him from the set and mentioned something about "a very grainy, out-of-focus shot of a very talented modern dancer."

"What's this talented dancer doing that needs to be out of focus?" Jeff asked, instantly suspicious. Although Jeff was always supportive of my artistic license, he was annoyingly prescient about my outright bullshit.

"Uh, he's, like, not, er, wearing any, what do you call them—pants?" I put forth tentatively.

"Sharon—" Jeff barked tenderly, "if I see a dick in this video, you're fired."

"I'll take care of it!" Matt assured me, instructing our male dancer to disguise his male member by wrapping it in a roll of ace bandages that we had borrowed from the assistant director's first-aid kit. After surveying the dick carefully, Matt applied the final artistic touches by encouraging its owner to roll it around in a little water, clay, and ground cover.

"Eureka!" Matt pointed with pride, as if a penis becomes less noticeable when it's five inches fatter and covered in twigs.

"Jesus. Now it looks like a big loaf of dirty French bread," I said bitterly. Apparently the MTV authorities, who referred to it later in their paperwork as a "cock-baguette," shared this impression. Luckily, Jeff changed record companies in mid-video, so he didn't have to fire me.

Okay, now over in the corner, all by herself, is a tall, ungainly young woman with a bad haircut, a strangely intense gaze, and Band-Aids plastered all over her arms and legs. That's Augustina, Mary Lambert's weird scary stalker-assistant.

"So you're saying that there isn't one single, solitary unmolted peacock in the whole entire world?" Augustina is yelling at the top of her very loud larynx. "What about Zanzibar? What about the Peoples' Republic of China? What about . . ."

Three weeks before, Augustina had told all the video staffers that she was in the final stages of Leukemia, but then two weeks later she told the commercial producers that she had AIDS, and then yesterday she told me that she had to have blood drawn from thirty separate spots on her body because she has site-specific hemophilia. Since Google has not yet been invented, I have no way of proving that Augustina is seriously mental, and Mary Lambert keeps insisting that she's just seriously committed to her job. Guess who's right? The last time I had sensed that an O Pictures employee was too crazy to work here, he got pulled over two weeks later with a hundred stolen credit cards and the torso of his recently vanished landlady in the trunk of his car. I did not furnish him with the character reference he applied for six months later from his cozy (permanent) cell at San Quentin State Prison.

As I approach the rear of the bullpen where the rock video executives are working today—their office having been co-opted for "Like a Prayer" boy-toy casting—I begin to tiptoe, hoping to catch at least one of them sneaking in a Tetris game on their new, company-bought, super-expensive hi-tech Macintosh computers, which look like adorable, old-fashioned television sets mounted inside hideous vomit-colored condo mailboxes.

"Well, okay, I did sleep with him, but I only *slept* with him. I didn't *have sex* with him." Taylor (Video Chick Number One) is saying to Rhea (Video Chick Number Two) as I sidle up. Taylor's job responsibilities include canvassing the music industry, schmoozing the directors, entertaining record company executives, getting us a lot of great jobs, and keeping our directors from dumping us for other companies that will schmooze them better. Her other skills include being hellaciously hot, wearing fabulous outfits, playing Tetris, and having complicated sexual encounters with inappropriate partners.

"Yeah you did," replies Rhea blandly, barely looking up from her computer. Although Rhea is Video Chick Number Two, she is slightly more interested in rock videos than rock musicians, which may explain why she will soon become Video Chick Number One, when Taylor runs off with a hairy Rolling Stones clone who has three wives and a husband.

"Well, okay, but I didn't have, like, *intercourse* sex," says Taylor, also barely looking up from her computer.

"Yeah you did," says Rhea, continuing not to look up.

"Yeah, okay, but it wasn't, like, in the honey wagon bathroom on the set. I mean, I know you think I'm disgusting, but you're *way more* disgusting, because you like Mötley Crüe and they have butt sex with sheep."

"Omigod! They're animal activists! There's no way they have sex with sheep," says Rhea, still not looking up from her computer, "in the butt . . ."

"Please!" continues Taylor. "They're the world's biggest douches! Nikki Sixx has overdosed on heroin and been clinically dead six times."

"Seven!" interrupts Veronica excitedly from across the room.

". . . and his swimming pool is in the shape of a vagina and I heard Vince Neil killed a stripper," continues Taylor patiently.

". . . and one of them ran over a box of kittens!" interjects Diana from her desk.

". . . and Tommy Lee paid the dolly grip on 'Don't Go Away Mad (Just Go Away)' two thousand dollars to eat a booger," finishes Taylor triumphantly.

Although it is a respected company pastime to exaggerate, embellish, or create from scratch repellent new stories that highlight the diabolical practices of Mötley Crüe members, the booger story had been eyewitnessed by members of our own staff.

"Shut up!" yells Rhea, finally breaking eye contact with her screen, which I can see now is completely filled with little blue and green boxes that are eating one another. "Whose booger?"

"Okay, I told you to stay off this new Internet thing . . ." I bust in on the ladies, who respond by frantically switching their computers to display budget sheets, as if they actually work for a living. "I just had lunch with that crazy-ass Rod Stovington, and he says he wants us to do two videos for a seventies hard-rock hair band that recently got upgraded to an eighties heavy metal band and they have two hundred fifty thousand for two videos and they want Egyptian pyramids, writhing slave girls, a pack of leopards running through a sandstorm, Nefertiti rolling around half naked on a sacrificial altar, and lots of guitar performance footage."

Taylor nods sagely while Rhea writes ferociously in a three-hole-punch notebook, proving once again that no one uses their computer for anything to do with work.

"*Hmmm.* For two-fifty, they'll get one video, all the guitar footage, a couple of camels, maybe one leopard, some really good runway models in chains, um, a decent desert storm and a cute little itty-bitty pyramid on a crappy Hollywood soundstage," muses Taylor.

"Whatever," I say. I have long ago stopped giving a shit about slave girls and men who wear gel on their bangs. "So what exciting good news do you have for me?"

The girls stare at me. They are actually dumbstruck, for once.

"Just kidding!" I relieve them after a couple of seconds. "You don't really have to give me *good* news."

"Jeesh! You scared me for a second!" pants Rhea. "Because here's what's happening: obviously we are in the middle of casting 'Like a Prayer' and that's going—"

"Sooooo shitty!" continues Taylor. "We still haven't gotten our first payment and we've already spent half the money and—"

"Madonna just changed her hair color to brown with red highlights so all of the platinum-blonde stunt doubles we've called in are useless," Rhea finishes.

"Also, we're having the expected budget problems with John Fogerty, because the record company doesn't want to pay for the dick reshoots, and we're having concept approval issues with Tracy Chapman, because no one can hear her voice on the phone. But the Metallica video is going great, as long as they actually show up for the shoot, which they never have before, so far."

Feeling a migraine touch down at the corner of my frontal lobes, I rummage through my bag for some mother's milk, I mean cigarettes, and find nothing but money, a comb, and ten empty books of matches. It's turning out to be a shitty day again.

"Robin-Robert!" I scream, calling out in a panic for my newly hired personal assistant, whose name definitely starts with *Rob* but ends with a syllable I haven't completely nailed down yet. Following a catastrophic series of hirings, I have instituted a firm policy of never learning my personal assistant's name until ninety days have passed without an incident involving drug hallucinations, felony assaults, or the stealing of O Pictures company toilet paper rolls. "Bring me a Marlboro Red!"

After careful in-the-field research, I have established cigarette brand dosages that correspond to accelerating levels of work stress, and this group of videos, plus the disgusting German zit soap commercial that's in preproduction, definitely merit something way stronger than Virginia Slims Lights.

"Gottdammmit!" Hildy is screaming as she talks on the phone with our latest utterly unpleasant, mentally unbalanced commercial director. "You have a filthy, most horrible cocksucking temper!"

As her face ripens to the exact shade of a Washington apple, I decide not to ask about the disgusting German zit soap commercial and instead duck cannily out of the room and hasten down the long silver-and-blue hallway that is swimming with gorgeous black faux saints. Then I notice my two male production assistants, Dickie and Hal, who are loitering outside the bathroom while they ogle a particularly fine fake Madonna.

"Omigod, that is so the real Madonna!" whispers Dickie with conviction.

"Dude, that is not the real Madonna. Look at her shins. Those are not Madonna's luscious, sinewy shins," whispers Hal with even more conviction.

"No . . ." says Dickie, "I really think those are her luscious shins. They're, like, really a lot muscular."

It fills me with sadness, irritation, and severe existential angst every time I see Dickie and Petey standing around, earning their (admittedly modest) hourly wage while they check out the legs on the ladies who are roaming through my halls. On the other hand, they're the only people in my office who've been willing to accept eight dollars an hour for fifteen years without asking for a raise. The moral of the story, which I won't accidentally find out for another fifteen years, is that Dickie and Petey are actually Hollywood's biggest celebrity pot dealers who are using their production assistant jobs as a front, so they can deliver product during coffee runs.

"Oh hey fearless leader . . ." says Petey, noticing me. As usual he doesn't bother trying to look busy.

"Hi boss lady," says Dickie, equally bored.

"Go get me some coffees and some paper towels, ASAP!" I bark at them, not realizing that I'm inadvertently enabling another non-medical marijuana delivery to another doomed movie star.

Moving past the accounting department and my personal yellow-and-green fake-marble office with the gold-framed, ten-foot-high billboard of Brigitte Bardot in *Contempt*, I enter the final frontier, the chartreuse-and-cobalt-blue fake-marble rock video room, packed with people, reverberating with music, and totally covered from floor to ceiling in Mötley Crüe posters, thanks to the predilections of my (silly, slutty) video staff.

"Okay, so you're a plaster statue of a saint in a small, inner-city church," Mary Lambert is saying to a shockingly well-built Christ figure as I enter the room. "And Madonna, who's confused and morally conflicted, comes in and she prays for your help."

"I see . . ." muses the actor, like he's studying Talmud.

Mary nods to me in a brisk, businesslike fashion, and I nod back likewise, as if we're both consummate, mature professionals who aren't in any way fantasizing about rooms full of gorgeous, well-built black men.

"Then she kisses your feet," continues Mary.

"I see," says the actor, nodding soberly, as if he's doing a serious internal character study instead of fantasizing about Madonna's mouth near his toes.

"Okay, and then you change from a plaster-of-paris statue to a real live man!" says Lulu, our casting person, who looks about twelve and is my only old assistant who got promoted instead of fired. "And then you escort her up to the altar!"

"That's cool . . ." says the actor.

"And then you pat her head and then you get on top of her," says Mary, "and then . . . you have sex!"

The actor seems surprised by this development.

"Whoa!" he stutters. "Okay. Wait a minute . . . so I'm a plaster saint in a church and I come to life so I can, er, uh . . . fuck Madonna?

"Yes," replies Mary. "Exactly!"

The actor chuckles nervously and then scans the room to see if anybody else is laughing. They're not.

"Okay," he says again.

Holding himself utterly still, he strikes the pose of a statue character.

"Lotsa attitude!" perks Lulu enthusiastically.

"Action!" calls Mary.

I think it's gonna be a good day after all.

The Sacred Time Line Leading to Me (and Rock Videos)

Ancient Olden Days	Ancestors accidentally discover music.
Way, Way Olden Days	Ancestors inadvertently become big Jews.
Way Olden Days	Big Jew ancestors boil chickens, dig up beets, and study tedious religious texts while growing unwieldy earlocks in shitty Russian shtetls.
1882	In an attempt to distract soon-to-be-revolting masses, Czar Alexander encourages Russian citizens to behave more anti-Semitically. Killing, raping, and conscription-for-life ensue.
1883	Oreck Ancestors attempt to evade Cossacks, outrun rapists, and dodge draft.
1903	Czar Nicholas endorses more killing and raping and lifetime drafting. More violent pogroms ensue. More evading, running, dodging.
1906-ish	Sharon Oreck antecedents finally hear about rest of world. Get the hell out of Russia. Travel steerage to Canada. Slowly pick their way to Los Angeles to take advantage of the clean air (not kidding) and wholesome environment to raise children in (also not kidding).

1917	Russian citizens unleash killing, raping, and oppressing skills on Czar Nicholas. Hah.
1929	Paternal grandparents set up housekeeping, buy fruit cart, and have three kids on initial five-dollar investment. Maternal great-grandparents do likewise.
1930	Paternal grandparents upgrade to grocery store. Maternal great-grandparents upgrade to deli. Dad of Sharon Oreck born.
1932	Sixteen-year-old maternal grandmother meets "Pickle Man," accidentally gets pregnant.
1933	Grandma marries Pickle Man. Mother of Sharon Oreck born. Pickle Man moves family to godforsaken Midwest.
1934	Grandma notices Pickle Man is mean, nasty, Midwestern, and (ugh) Catholic. Hightails it back to Hollywood. Remarries to mean, nasty Jewish fruit vendor.
1950	Parents meet.
1952	Parents marry. Twenty-year-old Mom accidentally uses diaphragm incorrectly. Mom accidentally gets pregnant.
1953	Sister accidentally born.

1954	Twenty-two-year-old Mom accidentally uses diaphragm incorrectly again.
1955	Me accidentally born. Family moves to fourteen-thousand-dollar tract home at 11620 South Chanera Avenue in the heart of Inglewood, California (phone number is Plymouth 44861).
1967	Family moves to Palos Verdes, accidentally making us the only Jews or Democrats within a hundred-mile radius.
1967	International Summer of Love.
1969	I start high school.
1970	I accidentally drop acid, have sex, and run away from home in the same week.
1971	I accidentally get knocked up in the back of a Volkswagen van.
1972–1983	See chapters 4, 7, 9, 11, 13, and 15.
1984	I accidentally produce my first music video.

2

The Ledge

t's April 10, 1984, and I'm talking quite harshly to two hundred crates full of stinking, blinking, steel gray homing pigeons who are steadfastly refusing to become fluffy, ivory-hued doves, no matter how much I threaten to pluck their tiny feathers.

Let me explain.

Six weeks earlier, I had abruptly decided to abandon my long-standing ten-years-in-the-making five-year plan to become a top-notch movie producer, thanks to my one-millionth dismal interview at a snotty major motion picture studio.

"Have you ever considered a more, uh, *creative* résumé?" the studio boss had inquired while fingering my credentials as if they had recently been in contact with a monkey butt. Because no matter what I did or when I did it, all anybody cared about was what I did it on:

My (Really Real) 1984 Résumé

- 1981, *Kill and Kill Again*: Dr. Horatio Kane creates an army of martial arts killer robots who take over the universe. His daughter, Kandy Kane, enlists a South African kung fu master to save the universe. Killing and rekilling of universe ensues.

- 1980, *Red Tide*: A complete dip-wad skin diver who has a dip-shit virgin fiancée who can't swim accidentally unleashes an old-school sea monster that only eats nonswimming, unmarried dip-shit virgins. Bloody body parts in murky salt water ensue.
- 1979, *Boogeyman*: A man full of boogey seeks artificially well-endowed nonunion actresses in order to impale them. Serial killing ensues.

Years of working on crappy, low-ball genre movies had guaranteed me a status in the motion picture industry somewhere just below a West Virginian pig fucker. Luckily, I was finally clued in to the professional loser's key to industry success: résumé hanky-panky.

"Of course, *I* would never hire you, but if you go elsewhere, feel free to, um, *elaborate* a little, dahling," the executrix explained in her fake English accent while booting me out the door. "Trust me, nobody calls up Oxford to see if you're really a Rhodes scholar. Ta."

Slam.

As Dr. Hannah S. Brinker—my brilliant but unconventional Dutch psychotherapist—has so often told me, "If you wanna be in showbiz, you gotta lay on the hooey."

With several strokes of my powder-blue Selectric, I had soon advanced my on-paper position from a boring, bleary-eyed assistant film editor to a fascinating, hot, hip producer who was entitled to professional respect, genuine recompense, and unmerited hissy fits. In the good old days before the international Interweb, lying, plagiarism, and résumé-enhancement were perfectly honorable business practices that couldn't be checked against all the kinds of pesky facts that are now available on IMDb, Netflix, and Defamer. Legends, after all, are born at that precise moment when 51 percent of the people you know have no idea who you actually are.

Besides, what was the big deal about producers? I had observed enough of them to know the drill:

1. Make a list of shit to do.
2. Hire a bunch of people to do it.
3. Yell.

After littering the halls of Hollywood with my pretend work history on nonexistent movies that had never been made, a well-meaning friend of mine told her loving, trusting coworker that I was somebody who I hadn't actually become yet. Accordingly, I got a call from someplace called Limelight regarding something called a "rock video" for somebody called Sheila E. Having no idea who, why, or what they were talking about, I immediately said yes. But before the production company could approve me, I had to be vetted by the director, Mary Lambert, who asked me to come over to her house for tea.

Mary didn't actually have any tea, but she did appear to have an income, or at least an attractive West Hollywood Spanish-style townhouse, a shiny new Mazda, and a classy French bidet with matching porcelain commode. That was several notches above my current standard of living, which included ten million black water beetles in my bathroom, a deteriorating American Motors Gremlin in my driveway, and an inherited fake-oak bedroom set that was manufactured right before Grandma starting forgetting which year it was.

"The singer is a sexy drummer who's either sleeping or not sleeping with Prince, who's her producer, who has a label at Warner Brothers," Mary revealed, unlocking the mystery of what a Sheila E. was.

Mary approved me as her producer, so I was sent on to my next interview with Limelight executive producer Simon Fields, who I was horrified to discover was a recent émigré from swinging London. My most recent fake résumé had me producing phony movies back in ye olde Englande for a period in the late seventies when I was actually collecting my welfare check in a concrete cottage in the Hollywood Hills. Lord love a duck! I was about to be revealed as the imposter I really was.

As it turned out, Simon was way too busy wheeling, dealing, and making up his own life to notice my wheeling, dealing, and making up mine. With his handmade shirts, prewashed jeans, and monogrammed deerskin slippers, Simon carried himself like a naughty billionaire who found the world of commerce just a tad below his class. Word was, he was either a distant heir to the Rothschild fortune or a former member of KISS, or he had made a fortune suing Dick Clark for a copyright infringement involving *TV's Bloopers & Practical Jokes.*

A guy like that was bound to respect creativity.

"Darling . . ." Simon explained while hurriedly scanning my résumé. "You seem totally upscale and professional, which is essential to the mission of this company."

Simon waved his hand around the eight-hundred-square-foot office, which was furnished entirely in black plastic, except for the single potted palm, which had been made out of green plastic sometime around the Kennedy administration. The lighting was fluorescent, the blinds were torn, the telephones were battered, and the single unisex bathroom had to be shared with the volatile hair-care customers of the neighboring Persian hair salon, who were inclined to shout loudly and in broken Farsi if the facility was unavailable for their immediate needs.

Seeing that Simon was an industry sophisticate, I decided to inflate my made-up salary to ten times more than I'd ever earned in my wildest imagination and then add 5 percent. It was well known in Hollywood that the more you ask for, the more you must be worth, and Simon was so impressed by my outrageous demands that he promptly hired me. He just had one question: Could I start tomorrow?

Du-uh.

As I sealed the deal with a firm and masculine handshake, a sudden sense of rightness began to swell my head with blood and entitlement. I was finally "above the line," a pulsing, five-foot-three hard-on looking to climb on and fuck the underclass. God, it felt good.

I immediately called home to share the exciting news with my poverty-stricken law-student boyfriend, Bill, who had moved in with me and my son, Josh (now twelve), four years earlier.

"Guys, I'm in! I'm going to produce something called a 'rock video' and I'm going to make something called 'money!' In fact, I'm getting three thousand, five hundred bucks!" Holy cash dollars—that was almost three quarters of my entire 1983 income, including Social Security taxes, food stamps, and free Virginia Slims from low-budget movie product-promotion deals!

"Good work, Mom. Can we get a house or a dog or a sofa that doesn't smell like Grandpa's furniture warehouse?" Josh asked plaintively.

My father's Office Furniture Emporium had donated our brindled living room sofa after a decade in the Bargain Storage Space, which had been invaded by a secret society of well-hydrated cats.

"Don't get all high and mighty, son! Gotta go! Love ya!"

Now all I had to do was, er, something?

Because now that I was a real, formally employed, paid-to-be-a-prick rock video line producer, I had forty-five minutes to make it to La Brea and Formosa, where a meeting had been scheduled during rush hour on a Friday afternoon in a dank, peeling, red-flocked conference room on the Warner Bros. Hollywood lot in the transvestite hooker section of East Hollywood. Why were we meeting in the ugliest room at the worst time in the world when no one was even working there? I had no idea and I would never find out. When you were dealing with Prince, there was never an answer, there was only His Whim.

As we gathered around a chipped faux-maple conference table to talk about what we needed to talk about, one thing became immediately apparent: this was a "music crowd." Those who had not consumed recreational drugs in the past twenty minutes were really wishing that they had.

No one was over thirty-five.

No one was *not* wearing sunglasses.

No one was driving a '75 cobalt blue AMC Gremlin that was an automotive hand-me-down from my Mom after she rolled it on Little Santa Monica Boulevard on her way to go see *Cats*.

Well. Okay. *Almost* no one.

Meanwhile, beverages were not offered. Canapés were not served. Everyone had limos to wax and materials to snort, so introductions were perfunctory and conducted by a nameless flunky in the style of a fight announcer:

"From Warner Brothers Records: Jeff Ayeroff! Head of creative affairs!"

Jeff was not "a man," he was "*The* Man," one of those guys who was not ahead of his time but ahead of time, period. Paid more than God to think like a speeding adolescent, Jeff could zip through ideas faster than a monkey with a remote control. He just didn't want to hold still long enough to execute them himself. Jeff *believed* in art, believed in music, and if you were really lucky he would believe in you too. The only danger was that his attention span would finish before you did. Slowness bored him. Bullshit bored him. Boredom bored him. It wasn't good to disappoint Jeff.

It made him, well, bored.

"From Limelight Production Company: Simon Fields! Executive producer!"

Mr. Fields was hilarious, handsome, and light enough on his feet to feign instant familiarity with whatever topic made its way onto the table, whether he actually knew anything about it or not. This was just the sort of quality I was yearning to emulate, so I set about watching him closely. Immediately I came to realize that the producer's main challenge in life was to project the appearance that he gave a shit about this video while procuring the next one. Check.

"Mary Lambert! The director!"

With her blonde, baby-fine locks and cornflower-blue eyes, Mary was a hipster ultrafemme from Arkansas with a yielding, buttered-grits accent that allowed others to view her as a wide-eyed doe while she ran them down with a ten-ton truck. At ninety-five pounds, Mary may not have looked like a brick house but she sure could act like one. In our hurried pre-job interview, she told me she had just shot her first professional music video for "Borderline," which I initially mistook to be a Mexican protest song. Hey, it wasn't my fault that my local Israeli Criminal Cable Dude had screwed me out of MTV just because my bribe check bounced.

"From the management firm Cavallo, Ruffalo, and Fargnoli: Steven Fargnoli! The manager!"

Steve was rumored to be a hit man for the Mafia, or at least he was supposed to be friends with somebody who knew somebody who was. Of course, so was everybody else in the music business with a vowel at the end of their name, but everybody said that Steve *really* was. No one could ever remember exactly who Steve had snuffed, but on the other hand, no one could ever remember the names Cavallo, Ruffalo, and Fargnoli, so at Limelight they were referred to as Salami, Salami, and Bologna. But not if Steve was around, just in case he *was* in the Mob.

Meanwhile, in keeping with the dictates of rock-and-roll etiquette, those from Paisley Park (Prince's recording label) were not introduced, because obviously Prince was so famous that it would be redundant. Unfortunately for me, the last time I had bought records was, well, before they turned into CDs and tapes. Before that day, I wouldn't have been able to tell Prince from Lassie.

Luckily, before I had left his office, Simon had filled me in on the Prince legend by showing me the "1999" video, in which

Prince occasionally emerges from a thick curtain of purple smoke to play peekaboo with his buttocks. With four-inch heels and his bangs slathered inches above his forehead in a unique Elvis/Afro bouffant, Prince appeared anxious to create the impression that he was over five feet three. Sadly, this was really effective only when four-foot-tall people surrounded him, which may have been the reason he was always firing his band.

In any case, here he was now with his raven-haired consort, Sheila, perched majestically at the head of the table on chairs specially laden with silken pillows, in order to better cushion their slender, well-muscled duffs. The splendiferous effect of their brightly colored clothing could only be described as Louie Louie the Fourteenth: purple fishnet, red pseudosatin, green-and-blue lace—and this was their day off!

Next to the rock gods lolled two large, gussied-up mack daddies who I assumed were Sheila's backup band, until they were introduced as "Clark and Riff-Raff," Minneapolis's answer to the house of Chanel.

"Clark and Riff-Raff are Prince's personal fashion consultants, who've been flown in to help develop a unique look for this rock video," Mr. Bologna explained. "We're fortunate to have them. They are talented artists."

Nodding proudly, Clark and Riff-Raff held up several see-through fake-fur teddies and a polyester brassiere that appeared to be modeled after human scar tissue.

"We are designing a look for Sheila that emphasizes both her timelessness and her modernity," explained Clark, while staring at Sheila's breasts. "Prince has also suggested we work with some of his favorite fabrics."

As dozens of bolts of fabric were proffered in a variety of synthetics ending in "-ester," I watched Mary blanch.

"Uh, Mr. Clark and Mr. Riff-Raff, this is all so glamorous," she began, laying on her Little Rock vowels while she got ready for the kill, "but I was just wondering if maybe you could do something kinda black, kinda like Armani, you know, with your own personal style, of course."

Misters C. and R.R., who were both dressed in body-hugging chenille suits that appeared to have been constructed out of purple bathroom rugs, glared at Mary as if she had just asked Picasso to paint a house sign.

"We don't do no shit like 'Marmani.'" Riff-Raff grunted with great hostility.

Then Prince, who had remained augustly silent throughout this exchange, suddenly spoke up.

Well, sort of.

Although Prince could sing really, really loud, he liked to speak really, really softly, so softly, in fact, that the collective table had to shut its mouth, hold its breath, and lean forward just to hear him at all.

"Sheila should have drumsticks on her pants," he mumbled.

For one outlandish second I thought Prince had said, *Sheila shouldn't have schlumpsters in her house!* Of course, it seemed unlikely that Prince would be employing Yiddish-tinged phrases to cast disrespect on our team, but what did I know of his strange Minnesotan ways? Then he repeated himself, just a little louder.

"I said, Sheila should have drumsticks on her pants."

"Omigod . . ." I whispered in awe, "special effects!"

I was no expert, but it seemed to me that applying poultry to a pant leg could result in unintended grease issues. Still, it didn't seem outside the realm of the Clark and Riff-Raff look.

"He means drumsticks, like you use on drums!" Mary whispered patiently.

"Ohhhhhh," I sighed, smacking my forehead. Sheila was a *percussionist*.

Abruptly and without another word, Prince got up, patted his bangs, and walked out of the building, followed closely by Sheila, Riff-Raff, Clark, all of the bolts of fabric, and the entire management team of Salami, Salami, and Bologna.

Mary and I stared at each other in horror, but the rest of the table remained calm.

"Don't worry, guys, everything is going to be great! I have total confidence in you and this music video," Jeff said. "If, however, Sheila does end up in this video with stupid drumsticks on her pants, I will bludgeon both of you to death."

Since Jeff's company was putting up exactly $35,000 in exchange for owning all the interplanetary rights (the term actually used in the WB contract) until the end of time to the "Glamorous Life" rock video, Warner Bros. would of course see that no felony charges could be brought against him.

"Important issues" thereby resolved, we spent the next nine minutes polishing off details regarding concept (Sheila leads the glamorous life, Sheila gets depressed by the glamorous life, Sheila gets laid), marketing (record should "cross over," from R&B—black people—to rock—white people), release dates (something impossible), and budget requirements (you get $35,000 and not one fucking penny more!), followed by forty-five minutes of really important stuff, like whether Sheila E. was Prince's girlfriend or his ex-girlfriend or never-his-girlfriend or a lesbian.

The correct answer was, who knew?

Because even if Prince had ever talked out loud and even if anybody had heard him, they had all been forced to sign confidentiality agreements promising never to reveal anything about him to anybody who might want to listen for as long as they lived.

Except me, of course.

Meanwhile, lacking further data, the meeting was formally adjourned, and Mary and I stepped out to get to know each other better. Maybe we shared common experiences. Maybe she understood what it was like to be different. Maybe she had had sex with her entire high school. Maybe she could explain what a music video was.

Two bottles of red wine later, I had the kind of epiphany one has after twenty-four ounces of fermented grape: namely, that before music television there had been just plain television, and before there was just plain television, there had been just plain music, but before they had gotten together to form their own network, there had been very little interest in merging the two.

Why?

Simple: the real purpose of television was not to entertain people, but to sell them shit they didn't need. Unfortunately, careful market research had proven conclusively that persons between the ages of twelve and twenty-five couldn't care less about aluminum foil, showed complete indifference toward color-enhancing laundry soap, and evidenced no personal affinity for expensive major appliances. Worse, they were too old for disposable diapers, too young for headaches, didn't have credit cards, and refused to see the upside of owing money that they didn't have. Why, teenagers were nothing more than stupid, lazy communists who couldn't even be counted on to purchase cigarettes, rubbers, or beer, the staple of the American beverage industry, fer chrissakes!

Positioned as they were between childhood—a sacred time of non-nutritious cheesy snack treats—and adulthood—when at last they could earn the necessary sticker price for a gas guzzling, U.S.-built luxury SUV—teenagers had been placed in the "wait-until-later" section of the vast programming market.

"Why should they get their own shows?" thundered the TV powers that be. "Let 'em watch *Bonanza* and *Tony Orlando* with their parents till they can spring for their own fuckin' Twinkies!"

In those days, there were only three networks, and although they were bloodthirsty competitors they all agreed on two things: keep any other networks (cable!) off the grid and avoid provocative subject matter (sex, drugs, rock and roll). What was good for General Motors was good for the nation, and what was good for the nation was maintaining the never-ending image-inside-the-image of a family watching TV while eating their Swansons while watching a family on TV eating their Swansons. And so all the networks continued to program into the seventies as if the teen and young adult demographics were a passing virus, viewing even the success of *Saturday Night Live* as a late-night aberration, suitable only for hippie misfits, sleep-deprived drug fiends, and peace-and-love nonconformist acid freaks.

Well open up, America, 'cause guess who was a-knockin'?

By 1980, those sleepless pinko stoners were precisely the material the new American viewing public was built of. No generation had ever been so attached to their peers and so withdrawn from their families. No generation had ever been so cynical about the present and so estranged from the past. No generation had ever been so isolated, so alienated, so stoned. Then again, no generation had ever been raised by Saturday morning cartoons, commericals for chocolaty nutritious Ho Hos, and a prime-time schedule in which, every night after their peer group was murdered in a foreign jungle on the six o'clock news, the network universe was immediately repopulated with wholesome young people who obeyed their parents, kept stuffed animals on their canopied beds, and reported all persons purveying illegal substances to the proper authorities. Rhoda was thirty. The Bradys were a bunch of dweebs. The Monkees were rah-rahs. The Partridges were geeks. The Mod Squad were narcs. Sonny and Cher were Republicans. That Girl had never even been finger-fucked!

Whatever was left of the rock and roll that managed to make its way down your antenna had been so thoroughly sanitized of its original content that it could barely inspire you to tap your foot, let alone burn your draft card or pull your pud. The words were changed, the volume was muffled, and even the sacred, pumping Pelvis of Elvis was stilled by the television powers that be!

And so the children went to their rooms, closed their doors, and cranked up their radios. Because jetting across the airwaves were the mysterious encoded signals from the prison planet Teen, secret messages of peace, furtive missives of love, and underground communiqués of evolution, revolution, and the new world order, all driven to the groovy four-four beat.

"We're right! We're cool! Fuck them!" crooned their transistors.

The kids were not alone. They were not insane. Well, actually they were. But that was the point: the networks may have been promulgating the voice of the reasonable adult, but radio had dropped by to tell them to shut up, because there was a new moon on the rise.

(Choir of angel voices up:)

And then there was cable.

The technology for cable had existed since 1948, but with their combined financial and legal resources, the networks had been powerful enough to lobby against it while successfully convincing the public that the whole idea was one great big communist plot. Then, sometime in the mid-seventies, Steve Ross, an enterprising entrepreneur who happened to be the chairman of Warner Bros., got a big idea.

"How do we get into this television thing? What isn't part of TV right now?" Steve Ross quizzed his people. "What do we *not* have that we *could* have?"

Television was exactly the box that Steve Ross wanted his company to think its way out of, so a tiny division (Warner Cable Company) was peopled with a team of bright young things from radio whose challenge was to go where no network had gone before—deep inside the adolescent mind. Meanwhile, the networks got a taste of some major corporate out-lobbying, and before you could say "free lunch for the FCC!" it suddenly became legal to be a cable station.

The fertile soil of music television had been left to be sown by television outsiders, entrepreneurs, radio programmers, and cable marketing mavericks who had a vision of talking directly to their own special demographic: teens. Well, okay, so the handful of people who originally cultivated MTV weren't really teenagers, but they were smart, confrontational, and ready for a brave new world, the kind of people who understood that every single American boy and girl really needed three little things: a little privacy, a little patience, and his or her own personal little network.

This was the eighties, remember?

After two generations of free speech, civil rights, and sexual revolution, teens were the final minority to make it to the speaker's dais, and they had something to say. Something different. Something nobody else knew how to say quite so well:

"I want my MTV!"

The collective unconscious of Generation X was a slightly different form of antimatter than what had come before it—altered, at a cellular level, by the caffeinated colas, cakes of sugared animal lard, and quadrillions of kilowatts' worth of cartoons and commercials it had managed to absorb in its formative years. These overfed, underexercised young people were the first true nestlings of television market research, a science that proved that what an inert child desired most from the television he was planted in front of was *movement*—the motion of characters across the screen, the rapid progress of plot, a change of frame, any pure and simple kinetic activity that could make him forget his natural instinct to explore the world. Quality in terms of production value, story, or characters was not the issue. People were willing to sit in front of any kind of simpleminded dreck, so long as that simpleminded dreck proceeded *quickly*.

But, ironically, it was that port in the storm of shit *Sesame Street* that would provide the subliminal structure for the MTV generation. Because from Monday through Friday, parents of the seventies had tried to offset the negative effects of television on their children by exposing them to . . . more television! Featuring a groundbreaking format of modular programming, the Children's Television Workshop was in the business of staying in business, and they knew what they were doing. For the first time, the kind of techno-psychology used to imprint "magically delicious" and "lemony fresh" was employed for something other than product placement. Television for the developmental welfare of children. Imagine.

Still, it wouldn't do much good if they didn't watch it. And what had we learned about entertaining the kiddies? Keep it moving! *Sesame Street* was to *Mr. Rogers* what Space Mountain was to the teacups. No one set piece on the show ran for more than three minutes; Big Bird, Cookie Monster, Oscar the Grouch, jumping rope in Brooklyn, baking bread in North Dakota—black, white, Hispanic, android—everybody got their turn, so long as it lasted no more than 2:59. And everybody sang: sang about their feelings, about being green, about being grouchy, about counting cookies. Twice a day, at nine and four o'clock, children across America from all walks of life became as one through the miracle of electronic bonding, eyes forward, butts down, millions of lips moving in sync as their favorite furry freaks sang and cavorted on a mythical street.

So when it came time to invent designer television for these children of "the Street," the network for "young adults" headed straight for the format already deep in the psyche of its audience: modular programming, featuring favorite characters singing about their feelings, three minutes tops, over and over, twenty-four hours a day.

With its media roots deeply planted, MTV launched its channel with a national campaign that urged the international everyteen to come forward and demand their MTV. Applying a daub of Maoist oratory onto the "I want my Maypo!" commercials of the early sixties, MTV tapped into the teen television unconscious and managed to serve some hot, bracing anarchy with its warm, hearty gruel.

The only problem was, there was nothing to play. It was all very well for MTV to go out and invent itself, but the channel had foolishly left the "programming" to others.

"You make it, we'll play it!" they tried to explain to the record companies, pointing to charts with bold, wiggly lines suggesting upward movement and untold profit. "Just like the songs on the radio! The people will buy records! It'll be great! You'll love it!"

"Hmmmm," responded the record industry. "Blow me."

Because as far as music executives were concerned, the whole MTV thing was a very expensive pain in the ass. Unless an artist demanded it, there was no way record companies were gonna feed MTV at their expense. Why should they pay for MTV? As far as they were concerned, they had already given radio a free ride for decades by providing broadcast material for bupkes!

For two years, while MTV explained, cajoled, wheedled, and begged, the burgeoning network subsisted on fewer than a hundred videos, half of which seemed to feature Rod Stewart shaking his growing heinie in a succession of ever tighter spandex pants.

Finally, in desperation, MTV stopped yapping and turned to a time-honored recording industry negotiation ploy: the conveyance from one hand to another of large piles of cash. Under the guise of "exclusivity fees" that promised to give the network first access to video premieres, MTV offered the record companies actual money for product.

"Music television! What a great idea!" crooned the record industry. "Why didn't we think of this? Let's shoooot!"

Heels screeching, the record industry executed an abrupt about-face. With the groundwork laid, and the piper paid, it was now mutually agreed that there would be a thriving business in music television.

"Let there be MTV."

And from this churning media miasma, new species crawled forth: music video directors, music video producers, and music video whatever-the-fuck-elses. Created in the image of MTV's brave new world, they were precocious, atrocious, and 100 percent totally unqualified.

Which leads me back to my vast experience with baton-twirling attire, video technology, and two hundred boxes of hoary gray pigeons pretending to be lithe white doves.

No knowledge, no problem. Professionals need not apply.

Lack of portfolio? Low prospects? Did I hear somebody call my name?

The Sacred Time Line Leading
to Rock Videos (and Me)

100,000 years ago	Humans discover ability to hum.
1800 B.C.	Abraham invents Jews.
1770 B.C.	Jews invent Cain.
1700 B.C.	Cain invents badness.
1600 B.C.	Cain's grandson invents first harp, leading to first association between stringed instruments and badness.
11th-century B.C.	Israelis invent professional musicians to work for recently invented royal family (leading to the term "royalties"?).
Ancient Greece	Plato begs the gods to reveal why all poets and musicians are crazy alcoholics.
The Middle Ages	Jews too persecuted to make music.
The Renaissance	Music goes classical. Musicians get money and chicks.
	Jews still too persecuted to make music.
1921	Crazy Mormon dude, Philo T. Farnsworth, dreams about inventing nuclear fusion in Salt Lake City but moves to Los Angeles and invents TV instead.
	Russian Jews get to America, finally unpersecuted enough to get into music business.
	Black artists invent ragtime and jazz.
	Black artists start getting ripped off by white record dudes.
1930s	Movie musicals become hugely popular, thanks to emotional depression due to economic depression.

1948	John and Margaret Walson invent cable television so they can sell television sets to people who live behind hills.
1949	P. T. Farnsworth realizes that huge corporations have co-opted his invention by stealing his patents. Goes bankrupt. Drinks self to death.
1955	Me born.
1956	*Rock Around the Clock, The Girl Can't Help It,* beach party movies, and first Elvis Presley movie released.
1960s	Networks encourage FCC to expand its jurisdiction so it can place restrictions on cable's ability to import distant television stations.
1964	*Hullabaloo, Shindig!* and *American Bandstand* hit TV, proving that music and television (sorta) mix, at least during the day. I go see *Hard Day's Night* on a double bill at the Rio Theater with *Frankie and Johnny.* No one stays to see Elvis.
1967	I get my first 45, "Itchycoo Park," by Small Faces.
1970	Cable interests fight network interests. Lobbying money increases with large corporate interests. Cable starts winning.
1971	Musician Mason Williams pitches *Video Radio,* a television program during which disc jockeys would play crazy-cool film clips to groovy music. CBS tells him to fuck off.

1972	HBO created. Cable begins in earnest. *Schoolhouse Rock* starts at ABC.
1975	Bob Pittman becomes the most successful radio programmer ever.
1977	Warner Cable launches first two-way interactive cable system.
1979	Warner Bros. hires Bob Pittman to come up with a music television channel.
August 1, 1981	MTV starts.
1984	Sharon Oreck produces her first rock video!

3

The Glamorous Life

t was time to roll up my sleeves and get down to work.

Unfortunately, there was no room to work at work. Despite a corporate appellation suggesting stainless steel warehouses teeming with vinyl-clad script girls and mohawked computer geeks, the offices of Limelight International Videos could only adequately be described as "dinky."

Tucked into a triangular second-story loft space, Limelight crammed five full-time employees, fifty freelance workers, and ninety broken video playback decks into eight hundred square feet of space. This wouldn't have been so bad if Simon Fields's office hadn't taken up four hundred feet of it.

Actually, Limelight was owned by a guy named Steve Barron, who had started it at the dawn of the eighties with his famous script supervisor mother, Zelda, and his famous groupie sister, Siobhan. With punk rock esprit de corps, Steve wrote and directed, Zelda directed and produced, and Siobhan produced and groupied. They were all successful in their chosen fields, but none more so than Steve, who in 1983 directed Michael Jackson's "Billie Jean" video, the first music clip to be scrutinized, analyzed, and dissected with the same insensible vigor as the Beatles' *White Album*.

"Look, man, there's, like, a *dude* under those sheets and, like, he's dancing backward, and there's secret Morse code messages in the flashing disco tiles!" prattled seventeen million fans as they swooped up the album like hula hoops.

For the first time, phenomenal talent, ferocious personal charisma, and a hard-driving repetitive bass line met up with a slightly complicated three-minute narrative form, producing an instant international MTV star. The timing was incredible—just as the perfect medium became available for a brilliant dancing pop star who couldn't act his way out of a paper bag, the most famous dancing pop star who couldn't act his way out of a paper bag showed up! Michael Jackson videos were to movie musicals what Starbucks is to coffee shops—quicker, cheaper, and pared down to the good part—the singing and dancing.

Jettisoning his years as a handsome and wholesome black child star, Michael Jackson had emerged in "Billie Jean" as a slim, fantastical, vaguely exotic mystery man, the kind of singing star you wanted to see while you listened to him. Following decades of segregated radio and television programming, Michael Jackson was the first crossover star, his creamy complexion spanning the great divide between R&B and rock. His phenomenal international rise fueled the success of music video marketing, and before you could say "seventeen million copies," pop stars were lining up around the Limelight block, screaming "Make me do the moonwalk, Steve!"

What had started as a lark was in danger of becoming a real live business. If this kept up, Limelight would have to purchase deposit slips, business cards, and stationery! Meanwhile, Steve was working all the time, so he recruited a bunch of new directors to work all the time, so then they recruited a bunch of new directors to work all the time. By 1983, with at least half their video business coming out of Los Angeles, Limelight decided to rent a trial office space where the operating policy was "cheap, cheaper, cheapest."

Still, what was important at Limelight was the sense of entitlement, the whiff of the future, the heady conviction that you were right there, on the cutting edge of the cutting edge, looking cool and holding the meat cleaver. An expectant, amphetamine-edged hysteria pervaded the scene, the sort of tension that demanded you keep your jaw wired and your eyes flitting back and forth, in case you were going to miss whatever was coming out of the woodwork next. The sense of being smack in the middle of what was "going on" was palpable. When you are in the right place at the right time, you just know you are there.

Unfortunately, everyone working at Limelight was haunted by the conviction that they had been hired in the right place and at the right time, but for the wrong job. The production manager insisted that he was really a screenwriter and the production co-ordinator felt she should be doing the production manager's job. The production assistant claimed he was really a producer and the casting person said she was actually an actress. The accountant wanted to be an animal trainer, and the producer's assistant was really a drag king who performed as James Brown at a lesbian bar called Peanuts.

Thanks to my feigned authority, ridiculous fee provisions, and recently made-up professional experience, I was the only Limelight employee who was grateful to be (over-) paid for my (undeserved) position. Sadly, my good fortune only encouraged my new coworkers to hate, loathe, and plot against me, especially when the staff accountant secretly passed around my preliminary pay stubs. Before I had even started my job, everyone at Limelight was looking at me like I was the blue-ribbon pig at the county fair—today a winner, tomorrow a hundred strips of bacon.

Meanwhile, it was time for bird casting.

Mary's script called for an unmolted male peacock standing around with a full tail fan. It also specified a large flock of white doves to alight on a deserted urban street and eat bread. This didn't seem to be an especially tall order, but every bird trainer I tried to contact appeared to be dodging my calls or claiming they were away on location. Although no one in the office would officially comment, it turned out that Limelight was already notorious in the eyes of the Hollywood animal-training community, thanks to an incident on a previous Prince video involving a cheap, stubborn (nameless) production person who had refused to consult a professional animal handler.

"Hah!" the cheap, stubborn, nameless production person had bragged to large numbers of bored, innocent bystanders after he went out and purchased a flock of Prince's favorite birds at his local discount pet company. "Some stupid trainer would have fleeced me out of thousands of dollars for 'training' these doves and all they have to do is fly. I mean, all they know how to do is fly anyway! You couldn't fuck that up if you tried!"

This turned out to be not exactly true, as he learned the hard way when he staged the first dress rehearsal on a working production stage by personally pitching the tiny messengers of peace right into the air. Immediately, the startled flock flew directly into a giant overhead fan, where they were promptly chopped, diced, and oscillated into great big gobs of greasy, grimy birdie guts, which were in turn splattered and sprayed all over the screaming and retching crew.

I suspect this incident was the inspiration for my third music video, the Prince classic "When Doves Cry." In the meantime, the subsequent investigation by the ASPCA strained Limelight's reputation among bird lovers. We needed an animal trainer.

Following extensive inquiries, in-depth studies, and tireless pre-Internet research, we finally found a second cousin of the first husband of Simon's most recent accountant who was willing to work for us as an animal trainer, despite Limelight's reputation as cheap-ass, go-it-alone birdie murderers. Unfortunately, two days before shooting, Creative Critters informed us that we would be receiving dirty steel gray feral rock doves—pigeons—instead of the agreed-upon pristine white American ground doves, who had suddenly and mysteriously become "unavailable until further notice."

"Not to worry . . ." the Creative Critters special consultant assured me. "These gray pigeons will look *exactly* like white doves, right after they are hand-massaged with organic vegetable dyes, tenderly rubbed with tinted lanolin, and brushed gently yet firmly in the same direction as their feather grain."

And our problems didn't end with pigeons; every peacock in the northern hemisphere had already molted by the time we got to our shoot day.

"I want a peacock!" Mary insisted.

"Sorry, miss. You can have a turkey, a vulture, or an emu, but you can't have the peacock because it won't have any feathers, because they already fell off," the Crazy Critters representative responded authoritatively.

"Can't we glue some on?"

"No, ma'am, we cannot."

Unfortunately, it was against PETA policy to use an industrial adhesive on a bird out of season, and Limelight had already used up its lifetime quota for animal abuse. No peacock.

On the financial front, the "Glamorous Life" video budget had been approved to include two fourteen-hour shoot days—one at the Wiltern Theater, one at an exterior downtown location, and one in the lingerie department of the old Bullocks Wilshire department store. Of course, I'm sure you can recognize that that actually makes *three* fourteen-hour shoot days, but back in the good ol' eighties, everybody in the accounting department was apparently too inexperienced, incoherent, or coked up to notice.

The day before we were supposed to shoot, Mary realized that she needed at least five vacuum-formed, Venetian-style, fourteen-karat-gold animal masks, of the type that were exclusively available at exclusive prices at exclusive sex boutiques.

"Well fuck you, fuck her, and fuck that!" the art director screamed when I covertly tried to slip the sex-mask duties into his department. "That's fucking wardrobe, it's for fucking tomorrow, and it's not in my damn budget!"

"I see what you are saying, dear," I said, attempting to placate him in gentle, soothing tones, "but I'm almost positive that a sex mask is a fucking prop."

As a general rule, I don't recommend cracking wise with angry crew members who are bigger than you, because they might be on steroids and lose impulse control just because you can't pay them any overtime.

"Besides," I added, trying a more conciliatory tone, "if you don't do it, I will have to hand it over to the fat boys."

Our Prince-ordained codesigners, Clark and Riff-Raff, had proved to be even more overpriced than they were incompetent, so I was constantly trying to pawn their work off on others who might not prove to be either. So far, I had snowed the choreographer into providing free leotards, told all the extras they had to bring their own clothes, and talked the limo driver into procuring his own chauffeur outfit. Unfortunately, the art director had attended a top English boarding school, so he knew when a big boy was humping him.

"Forget it," the art director replied, ending our conversation. "Get your own stupid masks."

I would have been more than happy to spend the rest of my day shopping for festive lion wear and avant-garde bear heads, but I didn't have time. I was to regret this later when an embarrassed production assistant presented me with a bill for $500, plus $50 in breakage fees from the Pleasure Chest on Santa Monica Boulevard.

"Sorry. I was reaching for the fox ears and I knocked over the glass dildos."

Meanwhile, call time for "The Glamorous Life" was 6:00 a.m., and I had to get up by 3:00 so I could show up by 4:00. As befitted my new top status, I was expected to get there first, leave last, and tell everybody how attractive they looked in between. This meant a lot of lying, but at least I didn't have to pick up the doughnuts, because the sacred morning meal had now been delegated to my laziest, most overqualified production assistant, who had recently graduated summa cum laude from a highly selective Ivy League university. As a general rule, it's always politically correct, emotionally rewarding, and incredibly entertaining to force overeducated heterosexual white males to sweep, mix Kool-Aid, and tidy up greasy snack foods. Then, if you are really bored and depressed, you can make them clean up the dirty napkins.

Our first day of filming was scheduled at the Wiltern Theater, where we would shoot the Sheila E. band members performing their hot new single inside a "magical golden pentangle" where they would be "bathed in columns of mystical, golden light." The performance footage, I quickly learned, was the bedrock of rock videos, as you needed to cut back to it whenever the narrative got too stupid.

While the cameraman and the crew that I'd hired at bargain-basement rates struggled to create golden, mystical radiance out of the prehistoric lighting kits that we'd procured for them at extremely reasonable rates, I was not surprised to learn that the first crisis of the day concerned Clark and Riff-Raff's "Glamorous Life" Sheila E. performance pants, which, despite ongoing pleas, entreaties, and threats from the record company, were still emblazoned from hip to ankle with shitty fabric cutouts of drumsticks.

Then we found out they were also three sizes too small.

"O mighty God . . ." I prayed as the sobbing wardrobe assistant tried to span the four-inch gulf of bronzed flesh that lay between the east and west sides of Sheila's weeping zipper. "Please look down upon us and help us get these pants over Sheila's tiny butt."

"I don't know how Clark and Riff-Raff did it," the costume girl wept. "Not even a four-year-old could fit into these clothes!"

It was true. Searching the length and breadth of the cavernous Wiltern Theater, I finally found the great and terrible designers hiding behind the video playback unit, talking about which Mercedes they were going to buy as they smoked a giant spliff.

"How dare you charge me five thousand dollars for this!" I demanded with great indignation, holding up a pair of lace and polyester toreador pants the size of an oven mitt. "There's not enough fabric here to make a cat yarmulke! I want your immediate resignation and all my money back or, or, uh . . . Jeff Ayeroff will kick your motherfucking asses all the way back to Minneapolis!"

Actually, Jeff Ayeroff was more likely to kick *my* motherfucking ass back to Minneapolis, but since there was no way he was going to show up on set before 10:00 a.m., I had at least four more hours to use his name as a threat.

"Okay, we quit!" the big boys announced in unison, and then abruptly departed. Perhaps they're still out there creating musical logos and Lilliputian pantsuits for itty-bitty pop stars—I don't know. What was important at the time was getting Sheila something to wear, because she had come straight to the set in her pajamas.

"Steve!" I said, calling over the Ivy League assistant who happened to be the world's youngest expert in medieval Japanese brush painting. "You have thirty minutes to find Sheila E. a pair of cool rock-star slacks in a size one, without any drumsticks on them, and don't fucking tell me that none of the stores will be open for six more hours."

"Oh God . . ." moaned Steve in horror. "A month ago I was studying Sesshu's fifteenth-century splashed-ink landscapes, and now I'm scouring the streets of Los Angeles for Sheila E.'s pants."

"Move it, zen boy," I curtly replied. "You can have one of your hoity-toity east coast existential attacks *after* you buy me a carton of cigarettes and find those pants."

With set crisis number one put off for the moment, I moved on to set crisis number two, an acute set shortage of white-flour breakfast products, thanks to Prince's eight-foot-tall bodyguard, Chick, who had somehow managed to wolf down the six dozen bagels we'd bought to keep the crew full until snack time. A film set is exactly like nursery school in that you must never be more than a half hour away from the next meal break or there will be meltdowns and people slapping each other.

After taking in Chick's gargantuan deltoids and large, richly inked iron cross tattoo, I decided to comp him the nosh and throw in some jelly doughnuts for good measure. He was crude, annoying, and a big, gluttonous wild boar, but he had really good gossip about Prince's clothes, sex life, and dysfunctional childhood.

According to Chick, Prince had been locked in a closet at an early age, which accounted for his obsessive need for control, his fear of strangers, and his compulsion to wear tight purple pants with holes that revealed his tiny buttocks. Of course, Chick was more of an ex–Hell's Angel than he was a certified psychologist, so I didn't really believe anything he said. Besides, even if Prince *had* been locked in a closet for three years, that was no excuse for buttless pants, not to mention purple buttless pants—not to mention pants covered with velveteen illustrations of drumsticks.

Meanwhile, if you ever watch the "Glamorous Life" video, you will notice that although the camera moves constantly from left to right and back again as Sheila drums, shimmies, and jiggles her drumsticks, the camera *never* actually completes a three-hundred-and-sixty-degree tracking shot around her. That is because the genius assistant quit his trouser-tracking duties, leaving Sheila's tiny drumstick pants to be held together by a giant yellow grip clip.

Other than the pants, the bodyguard, and the bagels, everything moved along at a brisk clip until dinner, when Burnt Offerings, the caterers that my super-experienced production manager had procured at a special introductory rate, showed up with the most disgusting food I've ever seen in my life.

"What in God's name is *that*?" I asked the Burnt Offerings chef.

"It's pork loin in a rich white sauce," he beamed.

"But you were supposed to provide a vegetarian option. Sheila, her entire band, and the director will not eat meat!"

"Yeah! Just like I said!" the caterer grinned. "This isn't meat—it's pork!"

After the caterer was fired, we sent Steve off to Maurice's Snack 'n' Chat for family-style vegetables for forty. Then, twenty more hours of work until we finally had enough performance footage to cover any conceivable narrative botch-up.

The next day, we had to be up bright and early to burn down a building. Well, actually, we didn't have enough money to burn down a real building, so we were going to burn down a tiny fake model of the building instead. Unfortunately, the model was still in the art director's car when it was towed away by the police, and he didn't have any money to bail it out, and I didn't have any money to bail it out, and they wouldn't take credit cards, which, as it turned out, none of us had anyway.

As a compromise, the camerawoman yanked out some two-by-fours from a nearby derelict building and then lit them on fire. Thanks to predigital technology, in extreme close-up and in very slow motion, those blazing yellow flames look exactly like a couple of burning two-by-fours that had been recently yanked from a nearby derelict building, but we stuck them in between a couple of shots of Sheila running down the street in a mink stole and panties, so we got five MTV awards anyway.

Listen and learn.

Finally, it was time to shoot to the action-packed Mardi Gras dance scene, which, owing to recent budget constraints, had been radically reduced from hundreds of professionally trained dancers, two peacocks, and a thousand fluffy white doves to six bedraggled art students, a hundred moth-eaten pigeons, and a filthy stray dog with a herpes eye infection. I went to go warn the bird trainer that we would be starting soon, and found him sleeping on top of a massive crate of pigeons who were very busy trying to kill one another.

"Hey, I only need a hundred of those birds and they appear to have gone psychotic and I thought you were going to treat them like little princesses and rub them with tinted emollients and they're still *fucking gray*, fer crissakes!" I whined.

"Oh yeah, I was working on that," the trainer lied boldly. "It's coming."

After I threatened to stuff a live gray member of the animal kingdom right down his dissembling gullet, the trainer promptly began squirting our pigeons with a white aerosol spraypaint, developed for old guys on a budget who felt a need to camouflage their bald spots. So much for gentle, loving animal massages.

"Why do you have so many of them anyway?" I inquired, gazing out at the sea of birds waiting in line to be shellacked with GLH (Good-Looking Hair).

"Well, you need two hundred birds for every take. These are homing pigeons, so they automatically fly home, back to Universal Studios."

"Hmmph," I grunted doubtfully.

Finally, at four in the fucking morning, the pigeons were ready for their close-ups.

"Okay!" the assistant director announced. "On my cue, the dancers will come forward and the pigeon-doves will be released to eat the bread crumbs."

"We've been training them to do this trick all month," bubbled the animal trainers. "They're very excited!"

It was true—the fake white pigeon-doves *were* excited. You could tell by the way they were trying to peck one another to death with their little beaks.

"Action, dancers!" yelled the assistant. "Let the birds go!"

On cue, the trainer and his assistant began swinging sticks, jumping up and down, and screaming very loudly at the top of their lungs. Then, all at once, in a mass bird panic attack, every single one of the spray-painted-white gray pigeon-doves flew out of their crates at the same time.

Apparently the bird assistant had forgotten to reaffix their cage latches after their dye jobs.

Whoopsie.

Up, up, up the little birds flew, rising like a massive feathery dirigible, until down, down, down they plunged, careening like a giant spray-painted bird-bomb.

Smack! The itty-bitty darlings splattered on the sidewalk.

Splash! They plowed into brick buildings.

Squish! They smattered onto our parked cars.

"Holy shit!" screamed the assistant director. "Cut the fucking birds!"

Actually, the birds did not need to be told to stop acting, as they were already lying around on the ground. It turns out that homing pigeons can't see in the dark.

Although I never received what I consider to be an adequate explanation of why professional animal trainers who were working regularly at Universal Studios did not know even one thing about domestic-pigeon husbandry, I did receive a substantial discount on the bald-man bird-feather spray. I would also like to add that while totally innocent pigeon-doves were badly wounded in the making of this video, there were no actual fatalities. Those pigeons were old school.

With great fatigue, horror, and solemnity, I called a wrap on my first official music video. We had been working for seventy-two hours straight, and due to conflicting schedules, I had missed the weekend, the laundry, the grocery shopping, and my twenty-ninth birthday. Mary said it was okay, because if you miss your birthday, you don't actually get older; but later, after she made me lose my birthday three years in a row, I made her buy me a color TV.

It was 8:00 a.m. before I dragged myself across my threshold to wish my son a good day getting straight As at school.

"How'd it go?" he said, grabbing the lunch bag I had recently filled up at the craft services department with their very last Kraft cheese slices, some smashed Fritos, and a crumpled pack of Oreos.

"Okay. Little rainy."

"Mom, I hate to be obvious, but under those kind of weather conditions, it's best to wrap out the exteriors and shoot the inserts," the little minx suggested as he left for sixth grade.

Throwing my disgustingly filthy clothes into the disgustingly full hamper, which was already reeking from the ash, pork, and pigeon shit embedded in all my other foul, unwashed laundry, I entered a hot shower, where I soaped myself and fell asleep for ten minutes. Then I awoke to towel myself with the three sheets that were left on the toilet paper roll, throw on my dirty nightgown, and make my way to the Grandma Rose legacy bed, where I laid my head upon my pillow to seek the sweet, sweet surcease of well-deserved oblivion.

Which is exactly when the phone began to ring.

Now, back in 1984, all the phones came from one phone company, and the only options available were black, white, or avocado. In that sweet, more innocent, low-tech time, there was no little doodad for turning off the ringer, there was no little gizmo to disconnect the wire, and I could not turn on the answering machine, because it had not been invented yet.

Ergo, on the forty-seventh ring, I decided to pick up.

"Fuck you, fuck you, and fuck you!" I screamed, remembering far too late that I used to have friends, a boyfriend, and a twelve-year-old child.

"Sharon, this is Joel Blumenau. Am I dreaming?"

Joel Blumenau was my rich downstairs nineteen-year-old neighbor, whom I had generously agreed to introduce to showbiz by allowing him to work for me for eighty-six hours straight as a totally unpaid production assistant, on the sole condition that he loan us his dad's no-limit MasterCard, so that we could put the security deposit down on the rental of the 1986 Mercedes convertible that Sheila E. needed to be chauffeured around in, so she could have casual sex with a complete stranger in the backseat (verse four, line six), so she could show that the glamorous life was either good (version one) or not good (version two).

Of course, this was back in the primitive eighties, when you still had to prove that you could pay it back before you were allowed to borrow money to buy stuff that you couldn't afford in the first place. Sadly, this meant that neither I, nor the director, nor the star, nor the owner of the production company had managed yet to obtain a MasterCard, even though we were all practically thirty and practically had real jobs. On the other hand, Joel had a big, rich daddy, so he was allowed to have all the credit cards he wanted.

"Joel, I am pretty sure you are not asleep at this time," I answered tentatively. "Unless I am asleep, in which case you need to get out of my dream and go home."

Joel immediately started crying instead.

"If I'm not dreaming and you're not dreaming, then I'm actually at the Chevron gas station on Beverly and Spaulding and I just went to pay for the gas and then I turned around and somebody drove off with the rented Mercedes, and my dad is going to have to pay Enterprise Auto Rentals a hundred thousand dollars because we left the card as a deposit, and I'm going to be dead, because he's going to kill me."

"Oh no, Joel," I replied soothingly. "I'm almost practically sure that the Mercedes SLC costs way less than eighty thousand, and definitely not more than ninety."

Actually, despite the fact that we lost my birthday, a Mercedes Benz, and several hundred cosmetically enhanced pigeons, most of the birds flew home, the insurance company ponied up the deductible, Joel's dad got off scot-free, and my budget came in at exactly $35,000, which is exactly what it was supposed to come in at in the first place. Well, actually, it came in at $35,010.45, but I threw in the rest.

The important thing was that I had faked it till I maked it, allowing me to become what I claimed I was already: a producer. When I was awake enough to savor it, I was filled with the possibilities for my future.

Maybe I was accidentally going to do something with my life after all.

4

There Goes the Neighborhood

When I was young, I was accidently impregnated on my sixteenth birthday in the back of a Volkswagen van by a conceptual artist known as "the Weasel" who had recently achieved local fame as the drummer in a band named Zazu Pitts. The Weasel had all the compulsory features of the really bad boyfriend, including a snarky affect, muttonchop sideburns, and the complete disrespect of all of his peers, so of course I was really attracted to him, especially when I heard he had a Shaggin' Wagon with a bed in the back.

I was committed to sex with jerks.

It was the seventies, a time of great social unrest, and in all the commotion I managed to confuse indiscriminate promiscuity with democratic engagement. The more unselective the liaison, I reckoned, the bigger the blow to the Man! This is a good reason people under eighteen should never be allowed to speed-read *The Communist Manifesto*.

April 10, 1971. It was the last night of Passover, Good Friday Eve, and my not-so-sweet sixteenth when Mark and I parked the van just outside Janice Costigan's Convergence of Great Holy Nights Dionysian Mystery Bacchanal and Brick-Breaking Party, where open-minded members of my local peer group had gathered to welcome in the vernal equinox by eating matzo, roasting

Easter ham, and divvying up a kilo of Acapulco Gold party pot into thirty well-apportioned five-finger bags.

The stars were out, the moon was full, and Jupiter was aligned with Mars. I can't prove there were mystical forces in play, but conception *did* occur at precisely the stroke of midnight, thanks to an unexpected encounter with the Weasel's mentally unbalanced ex-girlfriend, Cindy (the Psycho), who just happened to be out stalking the unlit cul-de-sacs of the Palos Verdes Peninsula while clutching an outsize plastic carrot.

A once renowned varsity cheerleader, Cindy had gone mental after learning that the Weasel was dumping her because she didn't put out. Of course, her reputation had been ruined; with virginity perceived in the seventies as forensic evidence of a stilted worldview, Cindy was condemned as a frigid she-fascist who was working to suppress the new world order by denying young men a proper sexual release. In those days, it was a well-known medical fact that a young draft inductee with unreleased semen blockage was in as much danger of blowing up as a Pinto in a pileup.

Dishonored and rejected over a once-valued membrane, Cindy had cracked just like my tenth-grade Ceramics 101 beer stein. Was the synthetic carrot that she clutched to her bosom an Ophelia-esque pun, a tattered love token, or a complex metaphor for the artificial nature of the school spirit industry? I never got to ask. While the Weasel and I were synchronizing our bestial rhythms to the classic second chorus of Spirit's "Animal Zoo," Cindy (the Psycho) circled the van, like a pep-leader bird of prey, until suddenly she pounced, launching her carrot like a Scud missile right through the van's open front window. There it splattered—*ker-smash!*—right on the Weasel's defenseless left butt cheek, where this very non-sixties act of aggression with a non-natural root vegetable provoked exactly the kind of convulsion that upset all of the Weasel's plans for an effective coitus interruptus and . . .

Unto me, a son was given.

Several months later I was on my way to the San Pedro Kaiser Permanente gynecological clinic after my mother finally noticed the pronounced swelling in my abdomen and decided to have me checked for a uterine tumor. I guess I should have told her by October that I hadn't menstruated since the previous spring, but ignoring obvious maternity truths was a hallowed tradition in my family, going back to my mother's mother, who had managed to get herself secretly with child forty years earlier, thanks to a condiment salesmen known to us only as "the Pickle Man" whom she met while working in the retail department of her parents' Hollywood delicatessen.

Impelled to marry in a hurry, Grandma had been similarly compelled to quickly divorce after discovering that the Pickle Man was a drunk, a skunk, and a secret practicing Irish Catholic who was scheming to move them all to Kansas, where he would baptize my infant mother. Promptly remarrying herself to a prominent L.A. Jewish fruit and vegetable vendor, Grandma managed to get accidentally impregnated five more times in a row before Grandpa number two ran off to go impregnate somebody else.

Twenty years later, my mother accidentally got pregnant herself when she was only twenty, on the first night of her honeymoon. To be fair, she had recently visited a qualified medical professional with the stated intention of obtaining a qualified prophylactic device, but when it turned out she was too embarrassed to ask how to use it right, she just used it wrong instead.

"Where in the hell does this goddamn thing go anyway?" I like to imagine my mother asking my father with a foxy, sidelong glance on their romantic first night together at the Pier Pike Motor Lodge in Long Beach, California. Since both my parents have to admit that I was the *second* little Oreck to be born accidentally in the mid-1950s, I am forced to consider that one of my parents was wearing a diaphragm on top of their head for at least half a decade.

Although getting knocked up young was clearly a genetic legacy, revealing my delicate condition presented certain technical obstacles. My father was a workaholic entrepreneur with a burgeoning office furniture empire and my mother was a psychologically brittle sixties housewife with a full medicine cabinet. Consumed with ignoring, sidestepping, or medicating their own problems, my parents made it very clear there was no room at the inn for mine. The Oreck family, they telegraphed succinctly, was a structure for attending twice-yearly religious ceremonies, Grandma Rose's Friday night chicken blowouts, and our annual two-week vacation in a qualified western national park. Messy feelings, ugly events, and distasteful experiences were things to be shared through the slamming of doors, the punching of holes in walls, and the waking of children in the middle of the night because the dishes hadn't been properly washed.

At my house, unpleasant personal problems were expected to be acted out, rather than acted on. If I could just suck up my Kegels and steal my mom's Playtex Living Girdle for the remainder of my pregnancy, a gleaming baby boy would slip out of my vagina and roll under the dinner table before I could be forced to fess up. Maybe by then I could figure out a way to blame the whole mess on my goody-goody big sister, who had developed the very bad habit of never doing anything wrong.

As it was, my casual admission on the way to the doctor's office that I might be, "like, six or seven months pregnant" prompted a burst of hysteria that I was discreet enough to interrupt only when I noticed my mother's gold Plymouth Barracuda veering straight toward an eighteen-wheel truck in the oncoming lane of the Pacific Coast Highway. This is an excellent example of the kind of consequence encountered when a "don't ask, don't tell" agreement is voided too quickly. Also, one should never break a long-term lying streak while traveling in a moving vehicle.

Meanwhile, after a forty-eight-hour period devoted to the marathon venting of shock, horror, and primeval rage, my folks elected to banish me to a foreign outpost before the community could take note of my ignominious condition. What they failed to take in was that at seven months pregnant everyone but them had already noticed. Not that our all white, protestant California beach suburbanite neighbors were surprised—as the local youth representative of the venerable Hebrew race, I was actually expected to behave like a jungle ape.

"Look, the little Jewess got herself knocked up!" the locals buzzed.

"Yep. Them folks are just like rabbits."

"Hey, that reminds me. Whatcha wearing for Easter?"

Haunted by the grotesque physical manifestation of a serious personal problem, not to mention the flaunting of my flawed moral structure in front of the goyim, my parents fell back on their belief that if *they* covered their eyes, no one could see *us*. Likewise, if nobody was watching, then nothing would have happened.

The plan was to place me in a hidden facility for the duration of my term, while my infant would be placed with a worthy white couple for the duration of his. Then, if I kept my nose clean and my trap shut, I would come home and they would redecorate my room in pucc. I don't think it coincidental that this was the one hue on the color chart that I summarily rejected.

I was dropped off at the first maternity home listed in the Yellow Pages, the Florence Crittenton Home for Unwed Mothers, which appeared from a cursory inspection of its edifice to be in at least its fifth decade of decline.

"We are not in the fucking mood for fucking comparison shopping!" my mother snarled when I suggested looking into alternative accommodations.

Perhaps it was the shock that accounted for her liberal use of the sacred and profane F-word, which only six months earlier had cost me a month's grounding, one facial smack, and two visits with my Mom's personal therapist—the sinister Dr. Malevant, MD—who offered to shut me up with a long-term prescription for the exact same tranquilizers she was always giving my mom.

Luckily, my community ties would never allow me to receive a mind-altering substance from a person who was not a teen-approved drug dealer in the greater South Bay area.

"Blah, blah, blah. I think I get the fucking idea," I muttered quietly enough to deny in a court of law.

"Oh my God! Do you hear the fucking mouth! Oh God! Do you see what she made me say?" my mother beseeched the Almighty with outstretched arms.

"Pul-leeezzzze, Dad," I begged, "don't you think we could look around a little?"

The Salvation Army's Booth Memorial maternity center was only a half mile down the road and supposedly had a wooden hot tub and a volleyball court, and St. Anne's Ladies Asylum, three or four blocks west, featured an open kitchen and unlimited rations of Mars candy products, or so it was rumored. Conveniently, all the unwed mothers' homes in Southern California were within a one-mile radius of one another and in the position of vying for qualified residents in order to hang on to their state funding. I was hoping to take full advantage of this object lesson in free-market capitalism, but my father would have none of it.

"This place is super!" he chirped, scanning the cracked concrete of the outdoor solarium, which featured a pile of dog shit and a rusted lawn chair. My father's facility for denial has always been of an Olympian nature.

"Anyway, Florence Crittenton is the best one—it's Jewish," my mother interjected, erroneously assuming that anybody named Flo must come from the chosen race. In times of trouble, my parents tended to yearn for the tribe they had moved to Palos Verdes to get away from.

"Mom, every girl here is Mexican or black, so I'm pretty sure they're not Jewish. Besides, what about all these 'others'?"

With Crittenton running third out of the three L.A. unwed mothers' facilities, the home had been forced to make up its population shortfall with girls who were not pregnant but had become wards of the state after being declared incorrigible by their families. Most were coming straight off a term at McLaren Juvenile Hall.

"I'm not used to being around convicts!" I cried, panicked. Visions of Linda Blair being ravaged by a toilet plunger in *Born Innocent*, the gripping ABC Afterschool Special on juvie chicks, flashed before my eyes. "I don't know the lingo! Everyone will hate me! I'll be raped by vicious young pseudolesbians equipped with stolen dinner knives and janitorial tools!"

"Well, you should have thought of that first!" my mother mused philosophically. "Anyway, you have no vote. You don't get to speak to us."

My parents kept trying to make it clear that I was in big, big trouble. What really chopped their block was my refusal to rat out the father of my child so they could pull out his nails, cut off his balls, and blame his parents for everything. Unfortunately, the Weasel and I were no longer on speaking terms.

Apparently, I'd been way too drunk to observe proper penis etiquette during the oral segment of our van love. Remember, I was still fifteen years old when the evening began. To be fair, however, the Weasel had been way too drunk to notice that it really hurt, and the pain certainly hadn't affected his fertility. Thanks to prompt medical attention, however, the Big Weasel's little weasel would rise again, unless my parents found it first and stuck it on a spit.

Meanwhile, the folks took my refusal to identify a specific partner as proof of a more universal paternity. As far as they could determine, I would deliver a tricolor litter of bastards, the multiple issue of three county high schools, a junior college, the San Pedro Masons, and the visiting Seventh Fleet.

I was nothing but a fancy woman, a slattern, a harlot, a jezebel, a whore.

Unlike my peer group, they refused to see this as a good thing.

"You have brought dishonor to our family! How will we tell people what you've done?" they keened, as if our clan hailed from some proud Norman dynasty instead of a bunch of slutty old chicken boilers. Under the circumstances, I felt it best to accept entry to the nearest maternity slum before the family elected to have me neutered.

5

When Doves Cry

The world's most tweaked-out video playback dude, who's got pinpoint pupils and is twitching and scratching while he's babbling and gibbering about obscure music minutiae that nobody else in the universe understands, is standing right next to the world's most annoyed rock star, who's wearing purple eyeliner and has a polar fleece G-string that's been cut down from Unionwear long johns so that his sensitive scrota sac will remain toasty and protected from unintended contact with aluminum folding chairs while he pretends to codirect the world's slowest-moving movie-related rock video.

Okay.

I'll tell you.

The world's most annoyed rock star is . . . Prince!

The world's most tweaked-out video playback dude continues to ramble on about ancient African rhythms, minor-key diatonic scales, and the mind-blowing recording techniques of the earth-shaking *1999* album while Prince just stands there, silently rooted, like a quietly aggravated purple turnip who has recently been outfitted with a winter-wear banana hammock. This only encourages the video playback dude to continue nattering on about his being the biggest genius in the history of human achievement.

"I'm not kidding, man, I need to know," he hisses as he begins to peak on whatever kind of designer amphetamine it is that makes you sweat and tic and be even more boring than a lecture on positive integers. "How did you achieve those awesome wah-wah pizzicatos on the English bootleg of 'Raspberry Beret,' man?"

With a distinctive lift of his expressive penciled eyebrows, followed by an imperceptible flick of his manicured left index finger, Prince beckons to Steve Fargnoli, his manager, who sprints across the set so that Prince can whisper something in his ear.

"Right!" Steve replies crisply, before beckoning to Simon Fields, who sprints across the set so Steve can whisper something into *his* ear.

"Right!" replies Simon, who beckons to me so he can whisper something into *my* ear.

"Prince told Steve to tell me to tell you to go tell that VTR dude to shut up."

"What?" I reply with outraged moral authority. Two feet away, the oblivious methman continues to shower Prince with odes to his brilliance, genius, and forward-thinking nudism while Prince just rolls his eyes and taps his foot impatiently. "He's standing right next to him—why doesn't he do it?"

"Because he wants you to do it. That's why."

As the kind of civic-minded, upstanding citizen who finds it reprehensible to have someone tell me to go tell an innocent video playback dude to shut up, I immediately make an executive decision to make somebody else do it.

"Pssssssssttttt . . ." I whisper to my production manager, Elizabeth. "Prince told Steve to tell Simon to tell me to tell you that you should go over there and tell that VTR guy to shut up."

Elizabeth looks at me, looks at Prince, and then looks back at me again.

"Are you crazy?" she asks incredulously.

"Yes," I reply with confidence.

Finally, after I promise to make a donation to her favorite environmental charity and let her go home sometime before three in the morning just because she's been working for three days and she's four months pregnant, Elizabeth politely asks the video playback guy not to talk to Prince, while Prince just stands around, polishing the halo over his head. Then the video playback dude stops babbling, walks over to a corner of the room, and starts crying. Then Prince gets bored and puts on some clothes and goes for a walk. His six burly bodyguards follow him and get arrested by a phalanx of Los Angeles Police detectives, who charge them with beating up a petite Japanese tourist who had the unabashed gall to point his Kodak Instamatic in the general direction of a five-foot-tall black man who just happened to be sporting a six-inch pompadour while strolling around in a seven-thousand-dollar white satin pantsuit and satin cowboy boots with eight-inch heels. Bail, as I remember, was buried as a grip-equipment overage.

It had all begun two weeks earlier with my very first message on my very first answering machine, which was as big as a sperm whale, cost three hundred bucks, and had come in a fake walnut finish with complimentary volume control, voice dictation option, and a plug. Immediately following the six hours it took me to figure out how to plug it in, a red blinking light began to flash furiously. Then, before I could run away in terror, I heard a voice.

"*CLICKergth . . . GRBL . . . is Simon Fiel . . . ggrph. Call me . . . ee . . . ase about a job imme . . . GLACK. CLICK.*"

It was way stupid and expensive and on the cutting edge of eighties home technology, but at least the money was going to keep pouring in, thanks to Mary Lambert, who had called the day before to ask if I wanted to go to Venice to produce "Like a Virgin" for her. Luckily, I was now so cool and hep that I actually knew who Madonna was.

"*Si, ciao bella!*" I exclaimed, hoping to sound like a seasoned world traveler. I'd been to Europe only once, on my 1976 Grand Poverty Tour, when all I'd learned to say in French, Italian, or

Arabic was "Please stop furtively masturbating in this bus/train car/squat toilet at once!" Although this wasn't likely to help me much on the Madonna video, as it turned out, it wasn't likely to hurt me much either.

"Hello, Simon?" I returned his call immediately. "This is Sharon Oreck, and I'm just *sooo* excited about going to Italy and doing the Madonna video for you!"

"Well that is just *sooo* sad," Simon replied cheerfully, "because you're not going to Italy or doing the Madonna video for me. I'm sure you'll agree that Mary should use an Italian producer since it is an Italian job. But don't worry—I have a fabulous opportunity for you, with a very experienced director, on a very hot video for *a major recording artist!*"

Actually, I had been left behind to produce another Salami, Salami, and Bologna production with big potential for small-animal abuse: Prince's "When Doves Cry." Apparently there was no escape from my twisted dharma path. But before I even had time to hear the concept, make a budget, or insert an anti–bird bludgeoning clause into my employment contract, I was informed that the entire infrastructure of modern civilization would collapse if I did not get to Steve Fargnoli's office in the next twenty minutes.

"It is of vital and immediate importance to Warner Brothers Studios that the clip for 'When (the fucking) Doves Cry' be completed promptly, as the (fucking) song got to number one already without any (fucking) marketing campaign!" Simon panicked as he pushed me past the bookkeeper's cubby on his way to shove me out the door. Obviously, if it ever got out that teenagers were determining their own musical tastes without benefit of huge-budget rock videos featuring skeletal Eastern European models with glossy Japanese-treated hair, literally thousands in useless advertising dollars would be lost.

"Um, I don't mean to hold you up, but who's directing this video once we actually know what it is?" I asked.

"Oh dear god—a director. I forgot!" Simon slapped his forehead. "Wait right here!"

Forty-five minutes later, Simon Fields returned to introduce me to a groovy young photographer who had recently been informed that he was a groovy young video director instead.

"Larry, this is Sharon, your fabulous producer! Sharon, this is Larry, your fabulous director!" Simon enthused as he shoved us out the door. "Now get out of here and make a video!"

I rushed Larry down to the car, careened out of the parking lot, and committed myself to several thousand infractions of the California motor vehicle code just so we could get to Steve Fargnoli's lobby right away, where we were settled like refugees for the next two hours.

"Do you have any quick ideas for a quick, fabulous video that could be done quickly and fabulously?" I asked Larry before I knew we would have enough time to rework Wagner's entire Ring Cycle.

"No, but I won't do it if there are any dead birds in it."

Larry had obviously done his homework.

"Well, what do you think about a little singing, a little dancing, and some montage footage of Prince driving around on a motorcycle with a gorgeous girl with large breasts?"

Since the song was featured in Prince's debut movie, *Purple Rain*, Warner Bros. Pictures had agreed to pay for half of the video, which meant we had to stick in at least *some* movie footage.

"Sounds good."

Plotlines settled, Larry and I got down to the hard work of reading five years of *People* magazine back issues until two hours later, when we were finally ushered into Mr. Fargnoli's office. Perched above a thirty-foot chunk of unpolished carrera marble that served as his desk, Steve conveyed the cruel authority of a mighty druid lord. Like the ancient mystery of Stonehenge, there was no earthly explanation for how that thing had been hauled out of Italy, onto a boat, and through his office door.

"Hi, Steve!" I tried to remain perky. "You probably remember me from the Sheila E. shoot . . ."

"Actually," interrupted Steve, "I have no idea who you are."

"Well," I started again perkily, "I am Shar—"

"Actually," interrupted Steve again, "what I mean to say is, I don't *care* who you are."

"Well, I guess you wouldn't be interested in discussing concepts then," said Larry good-naturedly.

"It's not that I wouldn't be interested," said Steve, "so much as I don't really give a shit."

"Okay," I said. "Should we discuss it with Prince then?"

Steve gazed at me pityingly before proceeding to relate the list of ground rules for dealing with Prince, Prince's people, or Prince's people's people:

1. Do not talk to Prince.
2. Do not look at Prince.
3. Do not ask why you cannot look at or talk to Prince.
4. Do not ask why you cannot ask why.

Amendments five through ten stipulated that any violation of the above strictures would result in a civil action not to exceed one bazillion dollars, unless you told somebody that you were being sued for one bazillion dollars, in which case you would be sued for two bazillion dollars. Interestingly, there were none of the usual video warnings about staying on budget, being on schedule, and sticking to the treatment, because there was no budget, there was no schedule, and there was no treatment.

"But how will I know where you want to shoot and who is in it and how much it will cost and how you want to shoot it?" I inquired.

"Uh, Prince will let me know what he is thinking and I will let Simon know so he can let you know. Meanwhile, order one of everything just in case," responded Mr. Fargnoli, before waving Larry and me out of the office.

As I exited his office, I noticed that I was gnawing on what would have been my last nailbed if I had had any nails left. Only recently I had been forced to guess exactly what a video was; now I was expected to guess *what was in it.* It was all very well and good for Prince not to know what he wanted, but I was the one who was supposed to have it ready in case he ever did! When Steve said to "order one of everything," did he mean one of everything *on earth*? Was I supposed to have a vat of Bosco Sauce, a troupe of dancing gypsy moths, and twenty-five pickled serial killer brains from West Texas standing by, just in case?

"Don't worry, Sharon," Larry, who had shot a couple of photography sessions with Prince, reassured me. "It's always like this," he claimed. "If worse comes to worst, we'll do the thing where he takes a bath and stares at himself in a mirror and crawls around naked on the floor. He likes to do that."

Several days later, the *Purple Rain* producers sent us a tangle of outtakes featuring Prince looking soulful as he drove around on a motorcycle, yelled at his movie dad, and made out with a big-bosomed actress who claimed that her real name was Apollonia.

"What am I supposed to do with this stuff? Do we put it in the video? Is it supposed to suggest content for the footage we shoot? Is it supposed to replace it?"

Day after day, I would pepper Simon to pepper Steve to pepper Prince with questions. Then Prince would tell Steve to tell Simon to tell me to stop bothering them but keep working. All our calls went unanswered. All our memos went ignored.

I rented a soundstage. I hired a crew. With Steve's approval, I ordered four different cameras, six different cranes, twelve different film stocks, and—despite Larry's vow—the requisite one hundred crates full of anxious white doves. Then, approximately fourteen hours before we were scheduled to start shooting, I received a message from Prince, via Steve, via Simon, that we should heat a large purple room with a big purple mirror, an old-fashioned Victorian bathtub, and lots of very, very hot water. Meanwhile, we could use the white background of a white soundstage to shoot the band, which at the time included a guy inexplicably dressed as a surgeon, a guy inexplicably dressed as a pirate, a guy inexplicably holding a mirror, and two beautiful lesbians who were dressed as—surprise!— two beautiful lesbians!

As with all of his acts, Prince's musical accompanists were required to dress like hookers, leer like buccaneers, and dance like a Broadway chorus line in very high dominatrix heels. They were also expected to constantly thank God for everything they had been given, especially their Grammys and MTV awards.

I had been dragging my twelve-year-old son to crappy film sets since he was four, but for the very first time, I was working on a crappy film set that my son actually wanted to see. Unfortunately, Prince told Steve Fargnoli to tell Simon to tell me to throw my own child off the soundstage after twenty minutes because he was convinced Josh was an industrial spy who had been employed by a rival recording artist to steal the music from his album, which, oddly enough, had already been released.

The truth was that working with Prince was a drag, a bore, and a disappointment. On the other hand, rock videos paid like a mutha and I'd just learned that there was a big price difference between Thunderbird and Châteauneuf-du-Pape.

Luckily, Mary had returned from Italy, where the shooting of "Like a Virgin" had come off without a hitch, if you don't count the sixteen-hundred-pound lion that had allegedly tried to eat Madonna.

"Is anyone on the set menstruating at this time?" the Italian producer had asked in Italian, since it was the only language he spoke. *"This is very important to know!"*

"Nope, not me!" said all of the Italian guys in Italian.

"Huh?" said Madonna, since she couldn't speak Italian.

"Bella!" said the production manager, signaling the Italian animal trainer to release the behemoth beast of prey from his steel cage.

"Sit-a-down!" ordered the trainer.

Fuck-a-you! roared the lion.

Waving his mighty mane, stomping his massive paws, and breaking his crappy leash, the fleet-footed beast padded straight across the Piazza San Marco, where, after a brief pause to adjust his trajectory, he re-aimed his large, furry muzzle *straight* at Madonna's uterus.

"Stop! Stop!" cried Mary.

"Mamma mia!" cried the crew.

"Arrrggghh!" cried Madonna.

Madonna spent the next ten minutes with the lion's nose buried in her mudflaps, saying things like "There, there" and "Niiiice kitty" and "Mary, I'm gonna kill you if I live through this!" Meanwhile, the king of beasts was eventually enticed away from Madonna's "Like a Virgin" area with a choice hunk of unrefrigerated horsemeat. Luckily, the cinematographer had left the camera running as he leapt into the nearest canal, so Madonna escaped with four new MTV awards and no loss of childbearing capability.

Meanwhile, I went on to no fame but some fortune (see chapter 1).

The video playback dude (whose name I could never remember) fell in love and married a woman who became a lesbian, so she dumped him for a chick. Then the video playback dude had a sex change so that his wife would come back, but then she stopped being a lesbian, so she dumped him for a dude. So now the totally amped-up video playback dude is a depressed and bitter video playback *chick*.

Simon Fields is the fancy-schmancy motion-picture partner of Jennifer Lopez. Steven Fargnoli died in 2001 of cancer while managing the career of Godsmack, an alternative metal band with a lead singer who was a devoted Wiccan.

Larry Williams, a gifted artist, family man, and filmmaker, also died in 2001, promoted to glory far too young by a congenital heart defect. He was lying under a tree, gazing up at the sun and some wild blue delphiniums, when his heart burst. The most beautiful thing I have ever heard in my whole entire life was the eulogy given to him by his twelve-year-old son.

Prince fired his band, then he hired them back. Then he fired our director. Then he fired his band again. Then he changed his name and then he changed it back again. Then he got married and said that he hadn't. Then he didn't get married and said that he had. Now, he is a practicing Jehovah's Witness, which makes him one of forty thousand people in all of human history who is actually going to go to Heaven, which, according to recent Watchtower brochures, looks a lot like the north side of Oahu, only it has lions.

1971 Packing List for Four-Month Visit to the Florence Crittenton Home for Unwed Mothers (and Others)

1. Seven extra-large white Mexican peasant dresses
2. Five packs of potpourri incense
3. Two hundred Reese's Peanut Butter Cups
4. *Siddhartha* in hardcover
5. *Be Here Now* in paperback
6. One bottle of patchouli oil
7. Seven pairs of "granny pants" maternity underwear
8. Two groove-worn copies of *Sticky Fingers*
9. One copy of Neil Young's *After the Gold Rush*
10. One copy of Joni Mitchell's *Blue*
11. Twelve odd assorted albums circa 1968–1971 (Simon and Garfunkel, Melanie, Spirit, Quicksilver Messenger Service, etc.)
12. One dinky beige-and-brown Panasonic portable stereo with removable speakers

6

What's the Matter Here?

It's four o'clock in the morning and I'm wearing a babushka, eating a banana, and riding Josh's old-school, twenty-six-inch-wheelbase skateboard across the pocked sidewalks of West Hollywood when I notice by way of an ear-piercing interstellar screech that a large alien spacecraft is hovering directly above me.

"Sharon Oreck, adjust the Fontana antenna, or the earth will be destroyed!" the saucer hisses at me from its outsize intergalactic space-speakers, just as the sky turns black, the pavement shatters, and a bunch of giant, fire-breathing lobsters start to dog-paddle toward Canter's Delicatessen atop a giant bloodred tsunami.

"Huh? Whaaat antenna?" I scream to the heavens, experiencing a brief but comprehensive blackout of qualifying verbs.

"Alpha, heat up that bubonic plague in Beijing!" barks the evil yet fabulous supermodel alien space chick captain from the floor of her sleek command module, where she calmly instructs her hot cosmic assassin squad on how to destroy the planet.

"Also, spread a super-tornado over to the whole northeast coastline of Canada! (*Ring ring ring!*) Beta, fuck up the Philippines. Epsilon, uhhhhh . . . melt an ice cap or something. (*Ring ring ring!*) And somebody answer that stupid phone! Now!"

"Whaaa . . . ello?" I wake up, receiver to ear, eyes twitching as I scan the horizon for the telltale shadows of flood, fire, and apocalyptic ash.

"Will there be fruit?" a teeny tiny mouse voice is trilling into the receiver.

"Wh-aat?"

I'm afraid. I'm confused. More important, I'm lying in the maple double princess bed that my grandma Rose gave me when she moved into the Home Shalom on La Brea and Melrose, and my husband is snoring, and the television is on, and somebody is whispering something about fruit into my left ear. In the meantime, how did a hamster get into my phone?

"Will there be fruit?"

For a moment, I consider telling this caller to eat shit and die for waking me up in the middle of a very important preproduction science-fiction anxiety nightmare. But if you want inviolate proof of how dumb my life is, I don't.

"So . . . are you asking me if there will be fruit?" I ask carefully. I want to get this right. I mean, this could *mean something*.

"Yes," the midget voice replies.

"Hmmmm," I muse thoughtfully, "*that* is an excellent question!"

Because although I am a rock video producer in a constant state of pretraumatic stress due to the ever present prospect of getting woken up in the middle of the night by complete strangers for no reason, I *always* find it prudent to pretend that I *know* what is going on, unless I *do* know what is going on, in which case I pretend to know *nothing at all*. This guiding principle provides the broadest opportunity to blame innocent bystanders for everything that happens in my life.

"It's not that I don't know who you are," I inquire cannily, "but—I'm just testing—*Who are you*?"

"It's me. Janet. Janet Jackson?"

"Oh shit!" I blurt out involuntarily. "I mean, oh, hi!"

I shudder violently as panic sets in, despite my Dutch postcognitive psychotherapist's recent injunction against proactive hy-pervigilance. Because it's not that I'm afraid, upset, or intimidated by Miss Jackson, with her adorable Minnie Mouse affect and sweet, postadolescent aspirations toward adult independence. No, it's more like I'm frightened of the cruel, dark forces that tend to muster around her, like her big, mean daddy, who recently suggested that he might like to kick my fat white ass around the nearest city block.

"Oh gosh golly! It's so nice to hear from you, Janet!" I lie vigor-ously, while slapping myself into consciousness. "I was just here in my warm, personal bed in the middle of a working night, at-tempting to put the finishing touches on your super-funky, totally today, pseudourban dance video 'Nasty'!"

Because in three and a half hours we are due to meet in a urine-soaked parking lot next to a roach-ridden hamburger joint in the middle of the worst-smelling, graffiti-wracked, butt-ugly barrio in downtown Los Angeles, so that the only girl in the world with a full-grown sub-Saharan African giraffe and a life-size re-production of the Disneyland Matterhorn in her backyard can dredge up enough street credibility to market pseudo-R&B rec-ords to the twenty million middle-class white children who yearn to be cool, poor, and black.

Meanwhile, there is the burning question of . . . fruit?

"Er . . ." she continues, "will there be fruit?"

"I'm sorry, Janet, but it's kind of hard to hear you clearly. Are you asking me if there will be fruit?"

Despite her ability to belt out a tune, Janet has a speaking voice that is muted and nebular, like Kipper, my mom's miniature Sheltie, who was compelled by a community injunction to have his vocal cords clipped.

"Yes, yes, will there be fruit?" Janet repeats insistently.

Hmmmm. Janet is obviously speaking in some sort of code. For a fleeting moment, my mind replays the scene in *Marathon Man* in which Dustin Hoffman is tortured with a sharp dentist's drill for incorrectly answering a question he does not understand. Thus I decide to proceed with caution.

"Well, yes of course, there *should* be fruit! Er . . . unless you don't want fruit . . . ?"

There is a long, pregnant pause, followed by complete silence. At least I think it's complete silence. For all I know Janet has dropped her voice a register and is singing the national anthem at the top of her little, whispery lungs.

"Janet, are you there?" I scream into the abyss.

"Yes."

Do you *want* fruit?"

"Yes."

"*When* do you want fruit?"

"Tomorrow."

"*Where* do you want fruit?

"On the set."

Well, now we're getting somewhere! But, in all things, especially those that relate to the comfort of celebrities, it's the minutiae that count. Think M&Ms, but not the brown ones. Think washing your hair in bottled mineral water, but not Evian. Think big green trailers that used to belong to Burt Reynolds, with full-length mirrors, a weight room, a steam shower, two satellite dishes, and a toilet with a flusher in front of you so you won't have to look down at your own feces. Yes, yes, I must delve deeper into the mind of a pop princess.

"So, Janet, when you say *fruit*, do I understand you to mean the edible kind of organic substance that, for instance, grows on trees or bushes, as opposed to some kind of symbolic *fruit*, that, for instance, accrues from productive toil? I mean, because obviously you would not be employing the disparaging slang verb for a male homosexual. I mean, would you?"

There is another long silence.

"Gotta go. Thanks."

Click.

Well, okay! Bye-bye!

I promptly pick up the receiver and start dialing legions of innocent below-the-line personnel so I can order *them* to wake up and go out and purchase bagfuls of fresh, nutritious fruit. Just to be consistent, I make my demands in a low, luxurious whisper. Then I hang up without saying goodbye.

"Hello? Will there be fruit?"

The idea of others resting comfortably when I am not fills me with impenetrable rage. Besides, an important facet of free-market capitalism is delegation, and I want to keep the American economy strong. Meanwhile, the tom-toms beat out the message:

"Hello? Are you there? Wake up! We need fruit!"

It's entirely possible that my highly paid caterer will show up on set tomorrow with luscious melons, juicy berries, and tangy tangerines. On the other hand, it's just as possible that Janet will arrive to find a wide selection of ham, salami, and headcheese, prompting Mr. Jackson to split my skull open like—speaking of fruit—a delicious, ripe cantaloupe.

Best not to leave these things to chance.

For some reason, the caterer and craft service person are not answering their business phones at four-thirty in the morning, so I make an executive decision to subdelegate all of my assistants to subdelegate all of *their* assistants to go buy produce, so by 6:00 a.m. there is enough fruit in Janet's Winnebago to tip it over.

What a triumph! I feel warmth suffuse my body as I walk on the "Nasty" set and realize I have survived the first cataclysm of my day with my tush impact-free. It is early in my career, so I don't stop to consider the implications of my self-worth's being tied to a celebrity fruit plate. To the contrary, I exult! I wallow! I am feeding Janet Jackson fruit!

By the time she arrives on set with her makeup-and-hair team, her six dancers, the choreographer, her mom, her break-dancer boyfriend, and all of *their* choreographers and boyfriends, I have decided that Janet and I are going to be *really* good friends. I mean, c'mon, I understand her. I get her. I know what she needs.

"Good morning, Janet! How are you today, little sleepyhead?"

"Mxxxlllphhhttt," she mumbles.

"Oh!" I reply, horrified. Janet has now made the leap from ridiculously hard to hear to ridiculously impossible to comprehend. "Yes. It was so fun talking last night, wasn't it?"

"Wxeritutreklfgri?" she replies.

"I see . . ." I continue. "Well, we've got a lot of delicious fruit for you in your beautiful four-bedroom trailer and—"

Slam! Janet and her glam squad enter their trailer and slam the door shut in my face.

Oh well. I guess we won't be good friends. At least no one has yelled at me or threatened my life yet, and it's already fifteen minutes into the day. Brimming with optimism, I execute a perky about-face and immediately run smack into the scariest man in the world, Mr. Joe Jackson.

"Oh shit!" I blurt, experiencing a strange déjà vu. "I mean, oh hi! I mean, oh, excuse me! I mean, er, hi, sir!"

Joe and his entourage of what appear to be thugs and cheap, ugly hookers all shoot me a vicious collective glower before turning their backs to discuss what a stupid white spaz I am. Nothing personal, but there's a contentious power struggle going on among every party on this video, so everyone is in a really bad mood, especially Janet, who's in a war with her manager-father—her manager-father who's at war with the record company, her mother (who'd like to divorce her father), and the choreographer (who'd like to get rid of Janet's boyfriend, but only because he'd really like to get rid of *her* first). Then there's the head of creative affairs, who really wants to fire the head of video affairs, because he is not properly dismissive of the head of the A&R department, although they both happen to agree about how much they hate Janet's dad.

Then there is the head of legal affairs, who is genuinely concerned that he might not get to sue the shit out of all of us by next Thursday, when he has to go on vacation in Barbados.

Meanwhile, I am the only one *everybody* hates *all the time*, for no reason that I can think of, precisely because I have *nothing* to do with *any of it* in *any way whatsoever*.

Let me explain.

Janet is famous, but she is not famous enough, because even though she is over twenty and has been on TV and has two gold records and is beautiful and talented and has been married and divorced, she still lives at home with her Jehovah's Witness mother and her tyrannical manager father, who probably tells her she's a fat, lazy slob because she doesn't move as many units as her superstar brother, who still lives at home with his crazy-ass chimp, even though he's twenty-seven years old and is a stone-cold bazillionaire who has a crazy-ass father who still yells at him for being a fat, lazy slob, even though he's sold sixty million albums.

Because it doesn't actually matter how many zillions you make, or the number of rhinoplasties you get, and/or how exactly you were able to squeeze a chimpanzee, six million gold records, and a full-size hyperbaric chamber into your own personal bedroom, you just will not flourish if the people who are supposed to bring you up are the same ones who intend to hold you down. Joe Jackson is a great big bully whose livelihood depends on his children not growing up, because the smaller they feel, the bigger he looks. If Joe's children ever achieve any kind of autonomy or self-awareness or professional hegemony, they will remember to fire his ass and replace him with a manager who's competent or polite or savvy enough to pretend that he might care if they actually live or die.

I have already had the pleasure of a direct run-in with Mr. Jackson at a "Nasty" video preproduction meeting that took place five weeks earlier in the bizarre Jackson family home. Buried low in the smoggy Encino foothills, the Jackson Hayvenhurst man-

sion stood out from its neighboring subdivision with a manicured two-acre stretch of sky-high green shrubbery that was
cleaved by a massive iron gate. Entering warily, Mary and I were
passed to a rustic stone path, which led to a charming cobbled
road, which led to a cozy brick cottage, which was surrounded by
some drooling attack dogs and a phalanx of uniformed security
guards wielding clipboards, walkie-talkies, and what appeared to
be 9-mm handguns.

All around us, delicate white and red tulips blossomed in the
middle of July, while pink baby roses bloomed mysteriously in
the hundred-degree heat. Meanwhile, chattering baby squirrels
frolicked with fluffy white llamas who darted among the South
Carolina magnolia trees that were twinkling in the middle of the
day with artificial lightning bugs. Perhaps it was the juxtaposition
of fake fireflies against a background of light artillery that caused
my abdomen to roil with the exact same nausea I experience
every time I pull into the Disneyland parking lot and remember
that instead of entering the "Magic Kingdom" I am just about to
experience bad food, long lines, intolerable heat, people wearing
giant bear heads, and constant, high-pitched exhortations to purchase an expensive plastic memento that will remind me of the
happiest place on earth.

Following a brief search and seizure, I was directed by a barking sentry to park my recently purchased gray Honda Civic right
next to the four Rolls-Royce Silver Phantoms that were parked
directly adjacent to the twenty-five-foot ivory carving of a fig-
leafed African American, which was right in front of the brick-
and-stone tract-style Jackson family mansion, which looked
exactly like a typical, all-American, mom-and-pop fifties house
on television—except that it had the same square footage as Lich-
tenstein.

From where we were parked, we could not see the legendary
on-site roller coaster, the mythical Chicago World's Fair ferris
wheel, or what was reputed to be the faithful reproduction of the

Main Street railway depot next to the swimming pool that was eventually relocated several hundred miles north when Michael bought Neverland Ranch when he was thirty-five. We did, however, spy a rare horned giraffe head rising above a eucalyptus tree just to the left of the house's fourth chimney. Later I was told by the head of video services that the giraffe got sent away to a wild animal refuge after it got diarrhea from eating all the palm trees, and the neighbors complained about the stench.

Meanwhile, a woman in a tidy maid's uniform greeted us at the door with a chewy brownie and a refreshing glass of lemonade before we were given a brief tour of the living room, which was as big as my dad's office furniture warehouse, plus the Pentagon; and liberally decorated with early American antiques that appeared to have been manufactured in the late seventies. From here we were briskly marched to the "record room," where the walls were lined from floor to ceiling with silver, gold, and platinum albums. Ignoring the inner voice that told me to run away before I was chloroformed and subjected to cruel experiments that would turn me into a compliant member of an aging boy band, I pretended to calmly sip my beverage while browsing through back issues of *Ebony*. Then I noticed a large *glass coffin* mounted in the corner next to the wet bar.

"'To Mr. Michael Jackson,'" I read out loud from an inscription at the head of the coffin, "from your dear friends at the Magic Kingdom." Inside, on a bed of pillowy red satin, sat eight tiny replicas of the animated characters from *Snow White and the Seven Dwarfs*. On closer inspection, I believed I could actually see them move.

"Holy bleeding Christ!" I whispered to Mary. "It's a plot! We're going to be turned into tiny Disney cartoon characters and have to live out the remainder of our lives inside a crystal casket!"

Patting me indulgently, Mary turned to greet Janet, who had just come into the record room with her wardrobe stylist and Paula Abdul, who was Janet's choreographer and best friend forever, unless Janet was really annoyed or mad at her, which was only 60 to 90 percent of all the time.

"Hi, Janet! How are you?" I asked.

"Imokayiguessithinkmaybe," Janet replied. In her pre-*Control* days, Janet was not really in touch with her feelings, let alone her vocal chords.

"Right, well then, let's talk about the vid—" Mary started to say, right as Janet's dad stomped into the room and slammed the door with his foot.

"*Who are you people?*" yelled Mr. Jackson, jabbing his finger at Mary and me.

On a good day, Joe was the rudest person I've ever met. To be fair, I was not at my finest as I slumped into the buttery leather couch and whimpered while trying not to wet my pants. This left poor Mary to have to stand up and greet Mr. Jackson with her usual southern grace.

"How do you do, Mr. Jackson? I am Mary Lambert, and this is Sharon Oreck. Thanks so much for inviting us to your home. We're really honored to be working on this project with you and your daughter."

As Mary extended her slender hand, Joe stink-eyed her in exactly the same way the coyotes on Commonwealth Avenue used to leer at my former cat, Stumpy, right after they realized she had only three legs.

"I am *not* happy to meet you," he replied, pointedly *not* extending his own hand as Mary sat back down again. "I don't like your work. Well, your Madonna stuff is okay, but I didn't want you to do this video." With refreshing candor, he continued, "I wanted a black director. But now that my daughter and the record company have made this decision against my wishes, I will do everything in my power . . ."

Here, for some reason, I actually expected to hear the words "to *assist* you in any way possible." I mean, wasn't it in Joe's best interests that the video be a success? Wasn't it way better for Janet to succeed than to fail? Wasn't Mr. Jackson ultimately a dad, and therefore always interested in seeing his own children do well and be happy and shine their inner artistic light for all the world to share?

". . . to wreck this video and get you fired!" Mr. Jackson finished instead. "Make *one* mistake, fuck up *just* once, and I will be right there, watching, waiting to mop the floor with you."

Janet ran crying from the room, and Paula ran after her, while Mary remained where she was and my bowels turned to polenta. It really looked like Joe was going to punch Mary in the face, after which he would punch me in the face, after which he would turn us over to the Jackson elves. For the first and last time in my life, if you don't count the flight I took home from Australia in 2002 when I ate cheap fois gras right before the seat belt sign went on for fourteen wretched hours, I actually thought I was going to poop in my pants.

Then Mary stood back up again. Even in her high-soled athletic shoes, she was about sixteen inches shorter and a hundred pounds lighter than Joe.

"Mr. Jackson, I am very sorry you feel that way. But Janet has asked me to work with her, and I intend to honor that commitment to the best of my abilities. I just hope that you find that meets your needs in the end."

As I prepared to curl up in a fetal position under the casket, Mr. Jackson became so unnerved by Mary's good manners that he choked and stomped out of the room, after which he proceeded upstairs to go break something, after which we heard a good deal of crying and yelling, after which we heard more stuff breaking and then some more stomping.

"Don't worry," said Paula Abdul, who had rejoined us. "He always does this. He's just jealous."

"Jesus H. Christ!" I said to Mary. "This family is almost as crazy as mine!"

The meeting came to a close shortly thereafter when Janet

came back down, blotting her face with Kleenex, and we all lied and told her that everybody's father was as scary as hers was. Then we talked about shoes, finished our lemonade, and high-tailed it as fast as we could out of the crazy, hazy valley.

"Jeeesh!" I said to Mary as we made our way through the billions of vehicles on the millions of freeways that are always being built so that people can get the hell out of San Fernando. "That guy is a prick. Maybe we should report him to Social Services."

Sadly, that would never happen. Because unfortunately for the Jacksons, what takes place on stage and television is not subject to the same kind of scrutiny as what happens in a trailer park or a sweatshop. Because if your next-door neighbor, Bob, mentioned to you that he was hard at work in the back office, managing his six little children whom he had working with pickaxes in a West Virginia coal mine, you would get together with some other families in the neighborhood to, say, report him to the police.

But when it comes to the Jacksons, well—nice work, Joe. Thanks for the memories. Have a cigar. Have 10 percent. Have ten more kids.

Watching the Jackson family back in the seventies (and their weird white doppelgängers, the Osmonds), we all wanted to believe that instead of sitting at home and eating Hamburger Helper and watching the Jackson family on TV like we were, the Jackson family was singing and dancing and doing the splits just like they would be doing in their own living room anyway. Because "that's not work, that's clean family fun! They probably do that all the time, anyway."

In the end, we see what we want to see, and what we want to see is the idea of hot chicks, the idea of cool guys, and the idea of wholesome family entertainment. We don't want to see the reality of predator parents who are exploiting their children in front of the whole world for money. Which is why Joe Jackson has been allowed to go through his children like a pig sniffing out truffles, putting them out to work until they quit or fire him, until now at last, it has come down to Janet, his last chance to dredge the cash up from his original investment in the human products of his loins (till he gets to the grandkids).

Which brings us back to the "Nasty" video set, where I have just run into Joe Jackson outside Janet's trailer.

"Good morning, Mr. Jackson! I hope you find everything to your liking! Can I get you anything?" I say, bowing and scraping frantically.

Mr. Jackson gives me his usual glare while jabbing his usual finger in the air. "Put the Cola in every frame."

He gestures toward a woman who appears to have been employed from a pool of local streetwalkers, and who is hoisting a six-pack of Joe Cola, a beverage that features the stern visage of Mr. Jackson with the inscription CREATED BY THE ENTREPRENEUR WHO CREATED THE JACKSON FAMILY on the can.

"Jeezus!" I reply, in shock. "I mean, gee, shucks, what a great idea! Looks like an excellent thirst quencher!"

I mean, gee, I can't wait to see Mary's face when I start shoving this shit in front of the lens.

Meanwhile, as Joe grunts at me sternly, I decide to take the high road and stop being so judgmental and just talk to him like he's a real person, with real feelings, who might not slug me if I don't slug him first.

"You know, Mr. Jackson, we've got some great fruit for Janet here today, and I must say, we really—"

I stop speaking abruptly as Joe puts his finger back in my face and shakes it several times.

"You make sure somebody shines up those cans before they go in the shot, ya hear?"

"You can be sure of that, sir. They'll be bright as a penny!" I promise, backing away as quickly as I can. "Boy oh boy! Did I mention that those beverages look refreshing?"

Omigod, did I just say "boy"? I run away and hide behind a pile of filthy hobos until Mr. Jackson leaves in his limo. Then I drop by the catering truck, where I see a gigantic plate of gourmet fine fruit.

"Heard ya went all out last night, sending everybody to buy fruit," the catering truck server chuckles. "We were bringing it all along anyway."

I get depressed. I eat a pineapple.

Meanwhile, as soon as it turns dark, every skanky, drug-addicted, cross-dressing male prostitute in Los Angeles County shows up at our location in full thrift store regalia and wigs. They are *not* coming to visit. This is where they score. This is where they whore. We are right at the intersection of East Seventh and South Main, which turns out to be the intersection of life and death and man and woman for the homeless transvestite population of California.

"Hey, baby! Where's your sistah, Michael?" screech the strung-out man-girls at Janet.

By midnight, the streets are seething with synthetic black-market estrogen when Mr. Moe, of Mr. Moe's Starlight Celebrity Bar, which is two doors south of our location, decides to organize a protest in the middle of the street.

"If you don't pay every one of us fifty dollars, we are going to flash you our pussies!" Mr. Moe screams, presenting his terms for a hastily assembled Union of Women with Adam's Apples.

Officer Bleary, the off-duty policeman I have enlisted from the payroll of the Los Angeles Police Department in order to facilitate traffic and provide security, immediately starts to hyperventilate and says he wants to call in backup.

"You can handle this, officer," I tell him. "It's just a big hissy fit."

"Yeah," Mary adds, backing me up. "They're just kidding. There's a long history of social humor in the transvestite community."

. Meanwhile, four men wearing black leather skirts hoist their hemlines and start kicking like Rockettes. They are not wearing undergarments.

"Eat this, Janet Jackson!"

Janet tries to pretend she's not there while our officer goes into panic mode and calls for a SWAT team. If there is one thing all of law enforcement fears, it's a woman with a penis. Ten seconds later, there are four cop cars arriving at our location with sirens wailing.

"Lady, I am shutting this production down until you can obtain adequate security and contain this, er, chaos," a lieutenant barks at me as he arrives on the set to find our dance boys doing a cha-cha routine in the middle of the street in their black-and-red leotards, while dozens of homeless cross-dressers try to impede them by dancing into the shot and dropping their panties.

"What are you talking about? Everything's under complete control here!" I protest.

"Puss-sssy! Puss-sssy!" the transvestites chant at the top of their lungs.

Hmmm. I try to keep talking to the cops while moving in an eastward direction, toward Sixth Street, while covertly directing Mary to continue shooting in a westward direction, toward Main Street. Unfortunately, a savvy vice detective, who threatens to arrest me, detects my ruse.

"Lady, what the hell do you thing you're doing?" screams the cop.

"Who, me?" I declaim innocently.

"Keep dancing!" Mary yells at Janet.

"Blow me! Eat me!" squeal the boy-girls into the camera.

"If you don't stop shooting right now, goddammit, I am gonna arrest, er, *this* guy and take him straight to jail!" the lieutenant screams, grabbing Bill Pope, who just happens to be the cinematographer, who just happens to be my new husband, by the scruff of his neck.

"Okay. Cut," I concede. I have to consider that Bill might really be annoyed and never have sex with me again if I have him thrown into a four-by-four cell with forty-five male prostitutes after having forced him to give up that stuffy ol' law thing so he could join me in the glamorous world of show business.

After an hour of peacekeeping negotiations, I promise the police that I'll hire ten private security guards who will work with us to control the streets in order to complete shooting. We are clear that we cannot move forward if there are any riots, any violence, or any men attacking the camera with their bosoms. In return for their cooperation, I agree to compensate all the street people with a total of two hundred American dollars, some really cheap fried chicken, and ten complimentary six-packs of Joe Cola.

Hallelujah! We have brought peace to these mean streets!

"We are very excited to be sharing in the rich cultural heritage of Mr. Moe's Starlight Celebrity Bar and the surrounding area!" I shout from atop a Moe's table. "Thank you for your support!"

I am rewarded with a hearty round of falsetto cheers.

Meanwhile, I tell all the production assistants to scour the community and offer fifty bucks to anybody wearing anything that vaguely suggests law enforcement. Thanks to a local pocket of fetish bars, we are up and running in less than an hour, allowing us to proceed with several important dance scenes that portray Janet as a tough chick who ain't afraid to throw down, especially with a bunch of fancy-pants boy dancers who look a lot more interested in baking cakes than in barking up her tree.

Our choreographer is Paula, the young and perky leader of the fabulous Laker Girls, a troupe of energetic, artificially enhanced young women who regularly fall over and perform upside down, revealing their spankypants in order to increase alcoholic beverage orders and swell Lakers T-shirt sales.

As a respected leader of leaders that cheer, Paula has proven to be a top-notch purveyor of super-peppy dance sequences, so our choreography consists mostly of hopping, squatting, clapping, and eye-rolling, mixed with the kind of pyramid fall that is really unpleasant for the men on the bottom. As a nod to the urban heterosexual who may not be that interested in seeing large groups of men skipping in unison while garbed in tights, Janet has also brought in some "street guys" who will enhance our video with some flash, up-to-the-minute, super-down-with-it "hip-hop choreography"—which turns out to consist mostly of hopping, squatting, and eye-rolling, mixed with some rolling around on their backs on the sidewalk.

By the end of the night, every member of the cast and crew is exhausted, fed up, and covered in a thick layer of unidentifiable stink. We are bloated, bloodshot, and blotchy. We moan, complain, and clear our throats like phlegmy old men. We have smoked one hundred packs of cigarettes, knocked back thirty quarts of coffee, and eaten two hundred pounds of the most disgusting fried foods ever created under God. We look like shit, we sound like shit, and we smell like shit.

Ho hum. Another successful shoot.

The director leaves. My husband peels off. The cast splits. The crew trickles out. By sunup, even the homeless prostitutes have abandoned the sidewalks to skulk off into their endless landscape of woe. The electricians roll up the cable. The grips load the truck. The production assistants sweep up the garbage. Once again, I'm left here with my loyal production staff to watch the moon go down on another abandoned video hulk.

Oh well. Everybody will be back tomorrow for another day of action, when MTV comes to shoot a video of us shooting a video, so that kids will think what we do is cool.

In the meantime, before I can get in my beautiful little car to drive home to my beautiful little bed, I decide to wander into Janet's mega-superstar rock video trailer and take a little peek.

And there I find it!

Shining, like the Ark of the Covenant!

Gleaming, like the Eiffel Tower!

It is the Biggest Complimentary Celebrity Fruit Plate in the Whole World.

And glory be its name! Every single one of its sliced Castilian blood oranges and its peeled Japanese sloe plums and its ripe Charentais summer melons and its sumptuous Beijing jujubes remains absolutely intact and 100 percent free of any kind of gustatory molestation. It hasn't been touched.

In an interesting video postscript, I get a call the following week from my friends over at the big rival production company Propaganda Films.

"Is it true that you guys started a total fucking riot last weekend when you were shooting downtown?" I am queried.

"Uh, no. Definitely not. Well, not really. Well, sort of. Actually, yes," I reply, torn between my deep desire to tell the truth and my deeper desire to avoid litigation. "But we are so sorry and we'll never do it again, probably."

"Fantastic! But could you tell us exactly where that was? Because we need to have a riot and get shut down for the next U2 video, and we don't have the money to stage it."

If you don't believe me, look up the video for "Where the Streets Have No Name" on YouTube, where you will find the band performing right above the exact same Republic Liquor Store where we traded a case of Joe Cola for a pack of Marlboro Lights at the end of our endless "Nasty" night.

Broken Land

t was on October 14, 1971, that I waddled through the
cracked portals of the Florence Crittenton Home for Unwed
Mothers and descended down, down, down her corridors of
woe, dragging behind me a frayed Samsonite Traveler into which
I had stuffed the twelve bare essentials for teen maternity conva-
lescence (see chapter 8).

Established at the turn of the century as a posh urban sanctu-
ary for the fallen daughters of the Pasadena elite, the Florence Crittenton Home had once catered to a steady stream of rich white
teenagers who would come there to pour tea, crochet doilies, and
read the Word of God while awaiting the inevitable consequence of
their falls from grace. But by 1972, the penitent white teen mom
had gone the way of the dodo bird thanks to the pill, the IUD, and
Puerto Rican abortions. Luckily for Florence Crittenton, the poor
and the ethnic were still around to pick up the slack—because the
lower the white-unwed-mother statistics plunged, the higher rose
their ranks among blacks and Hispanics.

And then there was me. As Florence's representative rich white
chick from the rich white sticks, I was really looking forward to an
authentic minority bonding experience. I mean, wasn't I a super-
bitchin' outta-sight universal-love pro–black power women's-
libber get-outta-Vietnam love-thy-neighbor hippie chick? Wasn't

this all one world, one great big collective love thing, regardless of race, creed, or color of cheating, faithless, prematurely ejaculating motherfucking boyfriends?

Not exactly.

Carefully laying out my miniature plastic stereo speakers in the downstairs recreation room on my first night, I set out to impress my new slatternly unwed mommy associates by firing up my most depressing Joni Mitchell song about addiction, loss, and unrequited romantic love. Back in Palos Verdes, this kind of audio gloom-fest had always functioned as a hipness flare-gun, leading way sensitive individuals to other way sensitive individuals, who could then be assured of sharing a common groove. I was promptly informed by Mo, a reedy African American who was alternately greasing and burning the shit out of her hair with what appeared to be a glowing tuning fork, that this was no longer to be the case.

"Okay. Now you listen, okay?"

Mo pointed a red-hot straightening comb at my much-used Joni Mitchell album.

"*That* is stupid white pussy shit. Okay? And *that* . . ."

Mo went on to indicate my entire album stack.

"*That* is *all* stupid white pussy shit! Okay? And I don't wanna hear no more a' your stupid white pussy shit! Okay? And nobody else does neither. Okay?"

"Well, okay," I replied dejectedly. By a clear majority of the ruling consensus, I was stupid and white, not to mention totally full of pussy shit, whatever that was.

As a cautionary measure, I looked around to see if anybody else was waiting to stab me with a grooming implement and stupidly locked eyes with Carlotta, a fury-driven Mexican American who just happened to have fresh blood and pus dripping down her arms.

"Don't even look at me, bitch!" Carlotta sneered. Perched on a ripped barcalounger, Carlotta was removing a homemade tattoo from her forearm by applying a lit Marlboro to it before stabbing it with a rusty stainless-steel razor blade. "I hear any more a' that fuckin' white pussy shit, and I kick your big white pussy ass around the big fuckin' block, too!"

"Right! No more stupid white pussy shit!"

I was anxious to appear cooperative, especially toward any large bad-tempered gangbanger chicks who had just gotten dumped by a faithless, no-'count ex-boyfriend with two first names, four middle names, two last names, and a gang tag. Besides, as a deeply committed pacifist (who was way full of stupid white pussy shit), I was not about to argue with any girl pointing a bloody cutting edge in my direction.

As I said goodbye to "Ladies of the Canyon" and hello to "Mr. Big Stuff," I tried to adjust my internal funk-o-meter to the very specific daily rhythms of the Florence Crittenton Home for Unwed Mothers:

6:45 a.m.: Hall alarm blares.

6:48 a.m.: Hoist body from bed. Clutch swollen genitals.

6:49 a.m.: Waddle to bathroom.

6:50 a.m.: Pee for 120 seconds. Wait. Pee again for 120 seconds. Wait.

6:51 a.m.: Repeat.

7:01 a.m.: Waddle back to room. Dress. Make bed. Smoke. Eat verboten candy bars. Search old *Life* magazines for pictures of people fatter than me. Smoke more.

7:15 a.m.: Drop by nurses' station to provide urine sample. Consider that no matter how much I've peed earlier, I still have twelve ounces left. Consider how much I hate staff gynecologist, Doc McNichols. Consider her big knuckles, her fat ass, and her frozen speculum. Consider flicking pee at her.

7:18 a.m.: Flick pee sample at Doc McNichols while her back is turned.

7:19 a.m.: Laugh uproariously. Waddle away promptly.

7:20 a.m.: Enter dining room.

7:22 a.m.: Eat copious amounts of Frosted Flakes.

7:25 a.m.: Eat ten strips of bacon for protein.

7:27 a.m.: Eat pound of hash browns for energy.

7:30 a.m.: Eat an orange because fruit is good for you.

7:40 a.m.: Smoke.

8:00 a.m.: Go to school. Fill out Social Studies workbook.

8:45 a.m.: Fall asleep at desk.

10:45 a.m.: Recess. Smoke. Get snack. Pee while eating graham crackers.

10:49 a.m.: Smoke more.

11:00 a.m.: Go back to school. Practice diaper skills on Chatty Kathy doll. Get lecture on not beating shit out of children. Laugh uproariously. Get threatened to have shit beat out of us. Agree to shut up.

12:00 p.m.: Lunch! Eat copious amounts of stuffed peppers, a pound of meat loaf, and a gallon of cheese soup with garlic bread. Eat piece of fruit for health. Eat bag of cookies for fun. Fall asleep at table.

12:20 p.m.: Smoke.

1:00–3:00 p.m.: Go back to school, fill out workbooks, sleep, snack, pee, pee, snack, sleep, smoke.

3:00–6:00 p.m.: Watch soap operas. Smoke. Snack. Walk to Thrifty and buy cigarettes and candy. Watch more soap operas, smoke, snack, play Aggravation or checkers.

6:00 p.m.: Dinner! Carb portions include spaghetti, potatoes, and bread.

6:09 p.m.: Have pie.

6:12 p.m.: Have pie again.

7:00–10:00 p.m.: Watch TV and smoke. Substitute *Jackson*

Five Show, Sonny and Cher Variety Hour, and/or wrestling at Olympic Auditorium for soap operas.

10:00 p.m.: Lights out. Smoke. Talk. Cry. Sleep.

Florence Crittenton was a vital place, but always at the cutting edge of madness. Since most of the girls had been humped, dumped, and brutally abandoned, mental health issues were rife and often acted out in a violent fashion. In an effort to avert incidents like "the Aggravation Game Rec Room Riot," during which seventeen residents were injured in a raucous, nail-scratching, head-thumping, bitch-slapping, bloody free-for-all over the question of who owned the lime-green game piece, an experimental weekly group "sensitivity session" was put into place by the powers that be. Presided over by a frizzy-haired hippie doctor, Ms. Leah Weissman, the first session began by bringing ten of us together to sit cross-legged in a circle.

"I'd like to try an exercise that would lead to some significant insights for everyone in this room," Leah said. "Why don't we try and say what we really feel about each other, in a open and honest way, huh? Remember this is a safe, nurturing place and you are free here to express your actual feelings!"

"Jesus. Fuck. Shit." We mumbled under our collective breath. Group therapy was probably better than school, but expressing actual feelings sounded way worse than the weekly five-knuckle pelvics.

"Okay, let's start with Felicia. How do we feel about Felicia? Remember to always start and end with something positive," Leah said. "Aretha, you begin."

"I think that Felicia is gross," Aretha offered.

Felicia was an unusually loud fourteen-year-old Caucasian girl who was not yet pregnant but was trying desperately to become so on the rare occasions when she managed to sneak out of the home. She was also trying desperately to be black.

"That's not positive," Leah chided.

"I can't help that she's gross. She has a forty-year-old boy-friend, and he's gross, and he's married. And she thinks she's a sistah."

"Fuck you!" said Felicia. "I don't have a married boyfriend, and he's not gross!"

"All right, let's go to the next person," said Leah hurriedly. "Elena?"

"I also feel that Felicia is gross," said Elena, "and I also feel that her boyfriend is married, and that she's not black."

"I agree," said Mo, the next in line. "Felicia is disgusting and white. But she has nice pants on!"

"Thank you, my sistah!" said Felicia.

The session went on like that until we got to the part of the hour when we were supposed to prove how much we trusted the group by telling a deep, dark secret. I learned quickly that the competitive spirit between people who have suffered abject abase-ment is just as powerful as it is among people who have experi-enced incredible achievement.

"Rebecca?" Leah would say. "What can you tell us?"

"Uh . . . I don't know," Rebecca droned, bored shitless. "I can't think of anything."

"Well, okay, would it be something like when your father broke your nose when he found out your cousin got you preg-nant?" said Leah.

"Oh yeah. I guess that *was* kinda shitty," Rebecca remarked, surprised you could get credit for that. He wasn't even a first cousin.

"Okay, thank you, Rebecca," Leah said gratefully. "How about you, Sharon?"

"Er, this Mormon down the street that I was babysitting for showed me his, er, wiener," I replied helpfully.

"Horrible!" said Leah. "That's really awful!"

"Thanks," I replied, blinking back crocodile tears. I was slightly awed by my powers of survival for the two seconds it took the F.C. girls to buck me off my high victim horse.

"Big fucking deal!" said Teeney. "Who hasn't seen a big ugly dick?"

Scanning the room, it became obvious that there was no one who had not seen a big ugly dick.

"Okay, Teeney. How about you?" said Leah.

"Well," Teeney replied, "I guess it would have to be when my stepbrother fucked me."

"Oh my God!" Leah freaked out. "Your stepbrother raped you?"

"Yeah," Teeney replied. "What you said!"

"No way, man!" Mo jumped in. My uncle fu— raped me!"

"Me too!" cried Jo Ann. "My dad! My real dad! That was not cool!"

"You're so right, Jo Ann. It was not cool. It was worse than not cool. It was an awful, hideous, terrible crime," Leah lamented, pale. "Let's take a moment to acknowledge that. To clarify that you are children who were taken against your will."

Encouraged by a psychological professional to "experience their feelings," the F.C. girls began to shriek, tear at their throats, and smash their newly distributed "sensitivity pillows" with a vigor that increased with every passing second. It was terrifying. I had never even heard of half the human indignities the girls in my group were bragging about having endured.

"I was raped!" "My dad killed my mom!" "My mom killed my dad!" "My mom killed my uncle because he raped my dad, who sodomized my brother!"

"Suck my dick, you whining little bitches! My father fucked me, my brother fucked me, my mother made me eat her pussy . . . So fucking what?" interrupted Carmen.

"Oh my God, Carmen," moaned Leah. "Is that actually . . . true?"

"Did you just call me a fucking liar, you fucking bitch?" Carmen bristled to Leah.

"Did you just call me a bitch, you fucking whore?" screamed Mo.

"Did you just call me a whore, you fucking bitch?" screamed Carmen while jumping up and starting to choke Mo.

"Oh my God! Please stop that! Stop that this instant!" Leah cried as the sensitivity session erupted in chair tossing, hair pulling, and serious hand-to-hand girl combat.

"Hey, everybody! Omigod, look! It's that guy from *Soul Train*!" I shrieked. "He's here! He's here! And he just went that-a-way!"

Thanks to a long-simmering legend that somebody at Florence Crittenton was distantly related to Don Cornelius, the baritone host of our favorite dance show, the girls froze like cats getting hit with a hose before offering a group hug and running out of the sensitivity session to pursue their dreams of television superstardom.

I learned something very important that day. Although misery, dysfunction, and injurious personal violence are inevitable parts of our misogynistic, materialistic culture, there is nothing that will heal a collective wound faster than the hope of pop culture.

8

Wicked Game

t's July 26, 1987, and I'm tethering Mick Jagger to an upright
aluminum folding chair in the middle of the night when Pete
Townsend asks if he can please go home because he's tired
and he has to get up early because he has an appointment in the
morning to record a seminal new album.

"Don't be a baby," I reply crisply. "We're right in the middle of
a frickin' Winky Dink!"

Mary and I had received a mercy invite to Mick's exclusive
forty-fourth birthday gala because he felt sorry for us because we
had been shooting a video for his solo album in London, and it
hadn't stopped raining for four and a half weeks. Meanwhile, I
couldn't bring my husband, because he wasn't invited, so I have
kind of been hoping the event would be a filthy bacchanal or a
drunken orgy, or at least a gaggle of fabulously good-looking
grown men wearing black kohl eyeliner and crushed-velvet dressing gowns while debauching themselves amid a sea of slow-witted
Russian prostitutes equipped with feather dusters, satin bolster
pillows, and meerschaum hashish pipes.

Ho hum. It turns out to be a ribs-'n'-chicken barbecue at Jerry
Hall's London townhouse, which includes all of Mick's family and
some of Mick's friends, who turn out to include most of the century's most famous rock stars and their dates. Mary has also

brought her sister, Blanche, who somehow managed to get through college in the mid-eighties without any exposure to illicit drugs, promiscuous sex, or any stupid pop songs except for "Hot Legs."

"Is that guy Rod Stewart?" Blanche keeps whispering.

"No," we keep whispering back. "That's Eric Clapton."

"How 'bout that one? Or that one?" She tries again and again.

"Nope, Bill Wyman, Pete Townsend."

"Who?"

"Yes."

"What?"

Never mind.

Blanche married a Lincoln and is now an ass-kicking U.S. senator from the fine state of Arkansas, which only proves that you can have a meaningful life by doing meaningful things instead of staying up late to take meth tabs in a hot tub with the pizza guy. Who knew?

Two months earlier, Mary and I had gone to New York to have a meeting with Mick and his manager, Tony, and Mick had been exceptionally gracious and Tony had been exceptionally kind, especially when I asked him if he could tell that the furrow just underneath my left nostril had begun furiously twitching just because Mr. Jagger entered the room and accidentally grazed my lower left elbow with his sensual right wrist.

Mr. Jagger was cute as lace pants, and Tony was the Cary Grant of rock, and Mary and I were excited and honored to be working with them, except for the time we took them out for wrap beer at the pub next to the Jacob Street Studios, where we ran into a hideously disfigured crazy female stalker, who had dilated pupils and pinstripe facial scars and the same aggressive brain damage as her hyperventilating German shepherd, who was foaming at the mouth while being dragged along like a battered rag doll on a very short leash that looked a lot like barbed wire. Somehow, Mick remained collected enough to talk his way out of being bludgeoned and buried in an unmarked grave while the rest of us sheepishly sneaked away so we could go hide in the limo and sip bottled beer while reminiscing about STDs in the seventies.

We were amazed to be invited to Mick's birthday party, because it was strictly a family affair—if your family just happens to include somebody who has been famous since ten minutes after he hit puberty. For the entrée course, I was seated with Mick's dad and brother, right next to Charlie Watts, whom I believe I bored more than any other single person has ever been bored from the beginning of all time. Then I accidentally mentioned my Scottish border collie, Jack Benny, and Mr. Watts perked up and we had a nice chat about *his* 950 untrained dogs for exactly the thirty seconds it took for him to be bored out of his skull again. Then I turned my attention to Mick's cheerful financial adviser, Prince Rupert Lowenstein, who promptly set to chasing me around the table in order to pinch my bottom, which he loudly announced was "good and plump" because it "had a good deal of meat upon it."

Thank you, Your Majesty.

Finally, after dinner, Jerry rounded up the whole party for a vigorous game of Winky Dink, which I will here describe, just in case you want to try it at home with your own group of celebrated pop artists.

1. Invite a bunch of famous rock stars and famous rock star wives to dinner.
2. Place aluminum folding chairs in a large circle.
3. Place a famous rock star in each aluminum folding chair and make him sit. Place a famous rock star wife behind each rock star and make her stand.
4. Leave one aluminum folding chair empty. Put a famous rock star wife behind that chair too.
5. Instruct the famous rock star wife who is standing behind the empty Winky Dink chair to scan the circle of chairs filled with famous rock stars and then wink at one of them

when nobody else is watching. (This is the "winky" part
of Winky Dink.)

6. Instruct the famous rock star who has just been
   "winky-ed" to bolt from his chair and try to proceed
   directly to the chair where he intends to be "dinked."

7. Instruct all the famous rock star wives to use blunt
   physical force to prevent the famous rock star from leaving
   his chair.

8. Watch hilarity ensue.

This game was so weird and twisted and confusing that it
lasted until 3:00 a.m., after which Blanche and Mary and I returned to our rented SoHo flat to discuss who had been the hard-
est famous rock star to wrangle. We all agreed that in general,
famous rock stars demonstrated a lack of energy and poor muscle
tone, possibly due to not having to work out in order to get chicks.
In the end, however, Mick's dad, a seventy-eight-year-old physical fitness instructor, was agreed to be the liveliest of the bunch,
although Blanche was disappointed that Rod Stewart never
showed up and had therefore been banned from competition.

Cut to 1991, on the big island of Hawaii, where we are shooting the video for another iconic male rock star, Chris Isaak, for
his song "Wicked Game." The shoot had gone really, really well, if
you don't count the part where we had to hike six miles in the
scorching noon sun after we forgot to load the camera or bring
any film or food or the director's glasses with us, so we had to go
back and do it all over again.

Then there was a tiny earthquake on the Chain of Craters Road,
and the Volcano National Park ranger said that we had better get
away from there fast, because we were standing in front of a six-
thousand-foot steam plume that was sitting on top of a 900-degree
lava bed built up from basalt, silica, and the burned-up carcasses
of dead Polynesian people, which had a tendency to destabilize
under shifting subterranean pressures, threating to plunge us off

the nearest towering cliff into the boiling, sulfurous pool of hot, molten magma that was lying directly below.

Then our top-tier Peruvian-Danish supermodel got a shard of obsidian impaled in her muscular left buttock and started to cry just like a baby, just because I asked her if she could do one more take of one more fake sex scene, just so we could finish the video and go back to our five-star hotel and take a Jacuzzi.

"You are so—how do you say it—'not sensitive,' and you don't even care if I am to live or to die!" she sobbed from the rear of our rental van, right before the location manager smashed it into the back of a Kona Island Police car and incurred a vicious tongue-lashing, not to mention a compulsory fine.

"That is so not true, er, exactly!" I protested violently.

Because to be honest, I do not feel comfortable bolstering the kind of degenerate culture in which people earn hundreds of thousands of dollars for loafing around with good skeletal structure while other people have to clean toilets just because they were born with abdomens.

What's important to remember is that the spectacular visual effect of Chris Isaak singing his heart out in front of a skyscraper-size eruption of billowing white smoke is, *in fact*, Chris Isaak singing his heart out in front of a skyscraper-size eruption of billowing white smoke.

Because we had been driving listlessly in our caravans on our way to yet another tedious afternoon of fit, attractive, half-naked people rolling around having depressed pseudosex on an exotic black-sand beach when our director, Herb Ritts, spotted a volcanic lava vent spewing out one hundred thousand cubic yards of blistering liquid magma, which hit the Pacific Ocean at a temperature of 943 degrees Fahrenheit, creating a colossal cloud of poisonous white vapor that rose like a mighty diaphanous fungus six thousand feet above the surface of the water.

"That's so great!" whispered Herb before taking off like a bolt from the blue, whereupon the entire crew waddled right after him with all our equipment, braving serious heatstroke and permanent lung damage caused by toxic fumes, hydrochloric acid, and minute particles of volcanic glass that the earth was disgorging into the air.

"Herb, I cut my knee and I think it's bleeding!"

"Herb, my asthma is acting up, and I don't have my inhaler!"

"Herb, I am getting perspiration stains on my polo shirt!"

"Herb, I cannot possibly carry these makeup brushes any farther!"

We never stopped whining on that long, sweltering journey to a black, flaming hell, while Herb never stopped ignoring us with his smug little smile. Because he knew, he just knew.

"I swear to God, it's going to be soooo great!"

So we just kept bleeding and gasping and toting those weary mascara tubes, because like the ancient Hawaiian warriors who had once followed the great king Kamehameha across those very same wriggling, smoking tectonic plates, we were just a bunch of feeble, pathetic chumps who were more than willing to turn over our fates to the kind of leader with a unique, personal vision who was more than willing to make all of us suffer in order to make some of us look great.

On the other hand, it had been considerably less expensive to follow a unique personal vision back in the great mid-eighties, before we could afford to pay depressed supermodels what they actually weren't worth to pretend they wanted to have sex with people they would feel more comfortable throwing a toaster at in the first place. In this vein, I would like to refer you to my first Chris Isaak production, the "Dancin'" video, which was shot on a patch of brown summer grass on a cold, cloudy night, next to a frayed red hippie tent that the art director had charged me a hundred bucks to filch from his own backyard. "Dancin'" also featured Chris's band (free), three fifty-dollar fake backup singers, some rear projection (free, my projector), some front projection (free, my projector), and an actress whom we had to pay $250 just because she was a professional actress who was Mary Lambert's best friend and had still not received her deferred salary from the last video. In the end, however, we managed to pull off the video with great style and panache, if that is what you want to call the 32D bullet bra that Mary made poor Denise Crosby (paid actress) wear for her gypsy fan dance on that balmy night when it was only thirty-five degrees.

The record company had initially approached me with another director, but then she and Chris didn't hit it off, so they broke up over "creative differences," which is what they call it when the first person thinks the second person is not as smart as he or she is and the second person thinks that the first person is a dick.

In more good news, Chris was anxious to create a video that conveyed the burning, yearning despair of an unrequited sexual obsession, so I felt totally comfortable introducing him to Mary, who ponied up with a fifties-style stripper, three different kinds of late-sixties film stock, and a psychedelic bull's-eye spiral that we could make out of construction paper, grip clips, and a C-stand.

Hired.

At the time, Mary was still vaguely under contract to Lime-light, but then they had a business misunderstanding, which led to bad feelings, general mistrust, and my producing Mary's next two videos via my own personal bank account. This had the direct result of increasing my yearly gross income from $7,000 to $107,000, which in turn had the indirect result of my getting an income, having to fill out tax forms, and decorating my house with a Panavision Silver Eagle answering machine, three plastic penguin wall hangings, and a lamp in the shape of a duck.

Because with 1984 had come my first disposable income, which I defined back in the twentieth century as any cash that was leftover after I had paid for half my family's food, half my family's rent, and all the three thousand cigarettes that I needed to smoke per day so I wouldn't have time to think about how broke I was. The rest was covered by my long-term boyfriend,

Bill H. Pope, who had recently quit his low-paying career as a starving cinematographer to take up a nonpaying career as a starving doctoral student who had to law-clerk all day in order to afford to go to law school all night, not to mention come up with half our housing and nutritional needs. All this worked out great for my new boss, Jeff Ayeroff, vice president of Warner Bros. Records, who was getting a bargain-basement deal by paying me more money than I had ever earned, mostly because he didn't realize what a cheap date I was, or he would have immediately paid me off in Marlboro Reds.

The Warner A&R people told Mary that they were determined to make Chris into the "male Madonna," which was not the last time a record company would try to make a pig's ear out of a silk purse. Because, even though Chris was mythically good-looking, could trill like a seraph, and had pecs and lats and abs and delts that were practically as toned as the walloping six-pack on Little Miss Madge, what made Madonna the queen of teen was her uncanny ability to reinvent her persona on an as-needed basis. Meanwhile, Chris always remained exactly the same person he had invented himself to be in the first place, displaying a singleminded facility for devising exactly the right look (Ricky Nelson meets Johnny Cash), precisely the right sound (Dean Martin meets Don Ho), and inimitably the right style (Tiki god meets Texas tenderloin) that would most effectively depict the Chris Isaak trademark feverish, haunted, lifelong love affair with total despair. As he told me on the first day of shooting, Chris could never completely relax, because the only person on earth he completely trusted was his mom.

Interestingly, it has been my life experience that whenever a man tells me that he's loyal only to his own mother, it's right before he says that he's also that loyal to me, which is right before he plants the bottom of his heel in the small of my back as I crouch without a parachute in front of an open hatch in a high-flying airplane during the middle of a severe thunderstorm.

Please see chapter 16 for further details.

Two whole days of production managed to pass with no heart-rending human tragedies, if you don't count the lunch on our last day, when I finally managed to insert my size-seven foot into my size-five mouth.

"Hey, Jimmy . . ." I complimented the guitar player, a gentle, slender man with a trademark Silvertone head o' hair. "Your hair is so thick and lustrous that it almost looks like a huge, hulking wig!"

"It is a huge, hulkin' wig, Sharon," Mary whispered to me, just as the guitarist skulked off to the bathroom to cry, and just as the costume designer came up to whisper in my other ear that all our hot backup singers were hemorrhaging like gunshot victims into their size-seven high heels.

"Damn, Sharon, my shoes *really* hurt," complained Misha, one of our gorgeous, six-foot-three, size-four über-unmodels, who was still only thirty minutes into the eighteen hours we were paying her fifty bucks a day for.

"Hey, me too, Sharon!" echoed the other reedy, six-foot, size-four unmodels, who were collectively receiving less money than our future Danish-Peruvian supermodel's left ear made per hour.

Following some low-rent, rock video–producer detective work, I made the bizarre discovery that every one of our tall thin actresses had big fat feet that she had tried to cram into black dominatrix pumps three sizes too small. Apparently there is a thinly veiled international conspiracy to convince long, skinny women that they should have short, slender feet, like the ones they used to make in China before those mean old Communists tried to force human beings to act all "equal." Luckily, here in America, we have plenty of altruistic people called "Hollywood plastic surgeons" who are devoted to helping poor, gangly-pawed supermodels cut off their elongated tootsies so they can finally fit into a size-four Manolo, so their feet will not clash with their truncated new noses, so they can better emphasize their additional maxibreasts, so they can better coordinate with their rejuve-vulvas, which have been trimmed, lasered, lifted, and siliconed so they will appear "younger" and "perkier," so people will think that they are "pretty."

In the meantime, there was nowhere to pick up three pairs of size-fourteen fuck-me pumps, so the backup girls performed in their stockings.

Actually, Chris Isaak was the only male heterosexual I ever worked with who would repeatedly claim that he *did not* want to have pretend video sex with a beautiful young supermodel. On the other hand, that is exactly what he had to pretend he was doing on "Wicked Game," and he didn't look *that* conflicted about it.

To be fair, Miss Denmark came to us at the continued insistence of director Herb Ritts, who firmly believed that the key to expressing one's inner beauty is to have outer beauty that looks twice as good. In fact, his approach to all things in film and life was the same: keep it beautiful and very simple.

"Less is more!" Herb used to repeat over and over, like a demented design automaton, until the day I asked him if I could apply that philosophy to his twenty-five-thousand-dollar-a-day shooting fee.

"Game" was actually the second video I had done with Herb, so we were still in our smoochy-woochy, whatever-you-say-dear phase, which meant that it would be at least eighteen and a half months before he would start asking for a 60 percent profit share while storming into my hotel room with a tape measure to make sure his suite was bigger than mine. Still, in 1989, Herb was already a big deal, hoity-toity, Condé Nast contracted, celebrity still photographer who commanded a massive daily fee, not to mention his library fees, his daily laundry stipend, and his "Akasha" Sikh catered lunch, including toxin-free tuna chips with Japanese soyannaise and organic spelt cream served on an exotic sand beach or a naked lakebed, preferably with northeast sun exposure.

Herb had the kind of cachet that led to the kind of comfort level that would allow major recording stars to feel cool about calling him up to say, "Hi, are you available to shoot on March fifteenth?" instead of waiting around for somebody to call somebody to call somebody else to make them call him. Which is exactly what happened on our first video together, when Madonna had inadvertently committed a class-five violation of the nineteen sacred steps (see chapter sixteen) by hiring Herb Ritts to do the "Cherish" video without calling her record company or personal management firm first. Because by simply opening up her phone book and choosing a number, Madonna had performed exactly the kind of unassisted dialing that leads very important music industry people to experience deep emotional pain, free-floating anxiety, and a deep, abiding desire to make somebody who looks exactly like *me* eat shit and die.

Why *me*, you may ask? Had I done anything wrong? Had I ever called a close personal friend and renowned celebrity photographer to come over and photograph me singing and splashing at the edge of the leukemia puddle formerly known as the Pacific Ocean attached to Malibu Beach? Had I ever canoodled and cavorted in an outgoing tide with an eight-year-old African American merboy while garbed in a wet, skintight black Calvin Klein sheath dress? Had I ever tried to upset the time-honored big-fish-eats-little-fish chain of music video command by challenging the God-given rights of countless music industry personnel to justify their questionable positions by putting in their two, four, or six cents?

Of course I hadn't. I was loyal. I was honest. I was a stupid, ass-kissing, sacred-step-subscribing sap. On the other hand, can you smell the aroma of sacrificial lamb that is wafting through the air? *Baa baa baa.* That would be *moi.*

Because as everyone who is familiar with the New or Old Testament can tell you, a close personal relationship with an all-powerful living goddess is maintained only through good communication, personal sacrifice, and close, intimate contact—if you haven't slaughtered your sacred cow, received stone tablets from a talking bush, or gotten yourself with child via your local holy spirit lately, you just ain't getting the Word on. Likewise, in the pantheon of the eighties divine, if Madonna hadn't called you recently, you had ceased to exist. Anybody could see Madonna—the question was, could Madonna see you? It hurt when Madonna didn't see people. Especially if they were very important people, like record company people or personal management people who were very used to not being ignored. Not being called made them feel invisible, unappreciated, and really a lot like breaking expensive lamps over other important people's heads.

But even very, very important people who yell at everybody else on earth if they don't get attention can't yell at Madonna, because yelling at Madonna will make Madonna unhappy, and when Madonna is unhappy, the manna will not flow, and when the manna won't flow, it means she won't be giving up a percentage of the gross manna to the very same very important people who can't get mad at her in the first place. Which is why, in the grand tradition of blaming the nearest innocent bystander, I will be yelled at. Yep, when it comes time to pay that piper, it will be coming out of my manna. Only on the "Cherish" video, I didn't have any manna, because I did it for free. This really made the record company mad, because there is nothing more annoying than a sacrificial lamb who is already dead.

It was my fault. The truth is that I had been trying to work with Herb since 1987, when he dropped by the set of "Open Your Heart" to shoot pictures of Madonna wearing her soon-to-become-signature armored corset with pointy unrealistic tit-torpedoes, which had recently survived a tempestuous fashion battle between a groovy French fashionista and Sean Penn, who had stomped off the set over the rejected blue velvet trapeze leotard that had come with matching turquoise fishnets and twelve-inch fuck-me heels.

Herb's pictures were always commercial, occasionally original, and every so often imbued with something dangerously close to grace. Even Madonna appeared to love him, and at that time, Madonna didn't appear to love anybody. Given Herb's clean, crisp style and celebrity-friendly reputation, I decided to strike up a conversation with him that would make me appear intelligent and interesting, or at least not as totally clueless about contemporary portraiture as I actually was.

"Wow, you trying out that new 5247 negative?" I carried on. "I hear the black tones are, er, super diffused!"

Like I knew forty-seven from schmorty-seven.

"*Hmmmppphhh*," Herb replied with subzero interest, having already determined through the trademark Ritts total body and soul scan that I was *not* a hunky, hot male model, a person of international repute, or somebody who was likely to make him more than forty thousand tax-free dollars in the very immediate future.

"Well, let's get together again soon!" I called out to him as he trotted off without acknowledging my existence, which he continued not to do until a couple of years later, when I was highly recommended to him one day by another of my directors, Matt Mahurin.

"Sharon, Herb Ritts got a Madonna video," Matt said, "and he keeps calling me for help, so I told him to call you for help, because you are the best and you are the greatest and I really love you and I really want him to work with you and I am not even kidding."

Now, all of my working relationships with all of the video directors tended to mimic the standard four-phase trajectory of a traditional Hollywood marriage:

1. Honeymoon love-ya phase
2. Maybe-I-could-do-better phase

3. Acrimony, recriminations, and don't-want-to-fuck-you-
   anymore phase
4. Dumping-the-shit-out-of-you-for-a-way-better-trophy-
   wife phase

After three years of working together, I felt that Matt was
somewhere between phases two and three, because he was acting
like a husband who knew his wife was going to cheat on him and
wanted to pick out her lovers in advance. On the other hand, it
was just one little video, so how much could it hurt?

"Madonna wants me to do something very simple that doesn't
cost very much," Herb told me at our first meeting, "so we have to
come up with something simple and cheap."

"Okay!" I countered with enthusiasm. "What kind of style or
approach would you like to take?"

"I'd like the style to be simple, and the approach not to cost
very much," he replied.

It was easy to mistake Herb for a complete doofus: he wasn't
articulate, he was obsessed with money, he was inconsiderate of
underlings, and he had only one idea. On the other hand, it was a
good idea: total perfection. Herb's genius lay in idealizing the ideal,
which in his mind came down to reducing something that was already gorgeous to its simplest, most geometrically pleasing shape.
However, if that simple, gorgeous thing wasn't in perfect, poetic
shape when he started, then, by God, it would have to be by the
time he got through with it. Even back in the primitive nineties,
Herb discovered complicated frame-by-frame graphics systems
that would allow him to digitally remove a furrow, a crow's foot, or
an ill-advised belt buckle that might be interfering with the integrity of a line. Herb once spent $10,000 removing a seagull that was
flying at least half a mile above Janet Jackson's bubble-do.

On "Wicked Game," Herb's quest for perfection took a lot of
people a whole lot of money to truck in a whole lot of planes with

gels, unguents, lotions, potions, powders, pomades, and goos to be applied to the one single person (Helena Christensen) in the universe who had never had a zit in her entire life. In other bad news, a large team of electricians, grips, and art department personnel had to be standing by 24-7 with huge arc lights, massive grip kits, and Greek columns, even though Herb never shot indoors or with artificial lights or with any prop other than a palm frond or a weather balloon or, every once in a while, a dead squid (see his famous "Djimon with Octopus" photograph).

Also, because Herb was fundamentally shy, he counted on others to relay important directing information, particularly when it came to matters involving basic human biology. Which is how I became Herb's trans-sex-slator:

EXT. – BEAUTIFUL TREE ON IDYLLIC BLACK SAND BEACH IN HAWAIIAN ISLAND PARADISE – DAY

Chris Isaak and the Danish-Peruvian supermodel are sitting in a tree. They are supposed to be k-i-s-s-i-n-g. They're not. They are tired, crabby, and sunburned instead. Chris wears a pair of shorts and a Hawaiian shirt. The Danish-Peruvian supermodel wears Calvin Klein men's underwear. Herb Ritts stands in front of them, looking through a director's eyepiece. Sharon stands next to him, looking overheated.

CHRIS
So will somebody please tell me what you want me to do?

SHARON
Herb, Chris wants to know what to do.

HERB
Ya know, that thingie we talked about before.

SHARON

Which thingie? The thingie where he yearns for her through his forlorn facial expression or the thingie where he tries to grab her tits?

HERB

Uh, no, you know, the thingie where he sorta, you know, yeah, and she should, just, ya know.

SHARON

Ohhhh. Okay. Chris, Herb says you should attempt to sensually feel the Danish-Peruvian supermodel's breast, and you, the Danish-Peruvian supermodel, must rebuff him in a way that says you both mean it and yet do not mean it.

HELENA

What means this, "rebuff"?

SHARON

Herb, Helena wants to know what you mean by "meaning it but not meaning it."

HERB

Uh, ya know. The hand thingie.

SHARON

Okay. Helena, Herb wants you to flick your fingernail polish and look bored.

Despite the tumult, the tedium, and the threat of hot lava, I attained a weird symbiosis with Herb on that video, which in some significant way marks both the highlight and the twilight of my rock video journey.

Because after it was all said and done, "Wicked Game" contained some of the most visually arresting images I've ever seen. The song is exceptionally powerful, but the video actually makes it more so, which is exactly what a video is supposed to do in the first place. As venal as Herb could be, there was something about him that was capable of the sublime. And when Herb saw what he wanted, then he knew what to do, and when he knew what to do, I wanted to do it too. Because even as I was moaning and bitching and am still sniffling and snarling about who did what and to whom, in the end I followed the leader. I did my job because he was doing his, and I trusted that if he thought it was great, maybe it would be great, and if it was great, I would be proud.

And it is.

And I am.

9

It's About Time

n addition to revamping my ideas about music, tattoos, and group psychological dynamics, the Florence Crittenton Home offered me a comprehensive reeducation in the nutritional value of cheese and pig fat, thanks to our four-hundred-pound assistant chef, Miss Olive, who considered any person weighing under 250 to be "a scrawny no-'count chicken."

"Eat like a woman, girl!" screeched Miss Olive, proffering a rasher of bacon–and–Best Foods–mayonnaise sandwich at my first breakfast.

"Yeth, ma'am," I replied, chewing cooperatively.

My fondest sense memory of Florence Crittenton re-creates eating peeled apple quarters on the rec room couch with Miss Olive and her scrawny, no-'count boss, Miss Winnie, who spent every afternoon from 3:30 to 5:00 p.m., watching Olympic Auditorium All-Girl Roller Derby. Thanks to their counseling in girl-on-girl skate violence, I was soon popular with the black girls, who considered the Los Angeles Thunderbirds to be the acme of modern athletic achievement. Meanwhile, Olive's high-salt-and-lotsa-animal-fat diet plan allowed me to contract toxemia, become prediabetic, and gain sixty pounds in a three-month period, and then to give birth to the fattest white infant born at the Cedars of Lebanon Hospital in 1972.

As the new sucker in town, I was initially assigned to a rank-smelling, chipped-paint dorm room with a girl named Rooster, who appeared to have severe clinical issues with Scotch tape. Although Rooster was almost wholly incapable of human relations, she had somehow managed to get knocked up by a handsome marine on a three-day port leave in San Diego.

"The s-a-x," she spelled out confusedly, "was soooo g-r-o-s-s! Do you like tape?"

After she wet her bed for the fifth successive night, it became clear that Rooster's interests had never extended beyond adhesives, so I petitioned for and received a new roommate, Ramona Remedios, whose personal assets included hundreds of relatives, step-relatives, and relatives of step-relatives and no overt inclination to beat the living shit out of me in the third floor bathroom like the rest of the Mexican girls at the Florence Crittenton Home.

"Why don' you call your mama to come pick you up in her Mercedes Benzedrine right now, you rich *puta*-ho?" the señoritas liked to taunt me while dribbling their cigarette ashes onto my head. It was not a good idea to be caught doing your business above the regularly patrolled first floor of the Florence Crittenton Home, especially if you had close relatives off the welfare.

Luckily, Ramona was unusually tolerant and quickly came to realize that despite their superficial trappings of wealth and privilege, my family was just as fucked up as everybody else's.

"Man . . ." Ramona sighed after my folks came by for one of their weekly therapeutic screamfests supervised by Dr. Weissman, "your people cuss worse than my cousin Freddy, and he has a fucking plate in his head from 'Nam!"

As Ramona enlightened me about life in the barrio, I shared with her my life on "the hill." I talked about metal bands and acid parties and she talked about gang orgies and quaaludes. In those magical days, any gaping cultural divide could be easily bridged by an illegal-drug anecdote.

Meanwhile, every Saturday we got to sleep in until 9:00 a.m., when Ramona's parents would come by to replenish our supplies of homemade Mexican treats and bring us up to date on what the crazy relatives were up to.

"So, your cousin Patty broke up with that *puta* Ramón, but not because of Antonio, because of Enrique. But Antonio didn't care, because he is going to marry your other cousin Patty—the one from Fontana—and Enrique, as usual, says he is getting a divorce from Lollie, but no one believes that shit but Patty—not your cousin from Fontana, the other one."

My parents, on the other hand, would come by on Sundays to remind me that I was a useless, worthless guttersnipe who would never amount to anything in any way whatsoever. In this vein, they had developed a plan for my future: I would spend one year being ashamed, after which I could rehearse being contrite. Then, I could devote the rest of my life to the good of our country by becoming a minimum-wage information operator for the Bell Telephone Company!

"If you do well, Stan's friend Chris can get you an entry-level position!" My mother beamed.

"I hear they have excellent benefits!" enthused my dad. "And you'll get discounts on long distance!"

Can you say, *What city please?*

Meanwhile, I was instructed to meet with qualified adoption personnel.

"Dr. Malevant says the Jewish agency is run by someone named Roth," my mother advised. "Here's her number. You'll talk."

When I went into Florence Crittenton, I intended to do as my parents commanded and give up my baby to a worthy childless couple. But the girls at the Home encouraged me to think again.

"Those adoption bitches are motherfucking lying baby pimps!" Rhanda, a veteran single mother on her second unexpected pregnancy, explained to me. "They will steal your baby and give it to Charlie Manson and he'll cut out its heart and eat it."

Besides me, Rooster, and a born-again Pentecostal from Arkansas known as Esther Third Trimester, nobody at the Home
would even consider giving their babies up to the kind of people
who were apparently available to adopt them. It was a proven
fact—or at least a widely disseminated rumor—that adopters
were unable to bear their own babies because they were physically deformed, mentally deficient, and inclined to sacrifice somebody else's infant to a red, horned Antichrist.

"If a kid was going to get stuck with a parent that freaky," explained Rhanda, "they may as well stick with us."

I wasn't so sure. Because of the Florence Crittenton antiadop-
tion stance, I had already been besieged by agencies that all assured me my child would be better off without me. At no time in
my life, before or since, have I been treated so much like a T-bone
in a kennel full of rottweilers. Finally, I settled on the Children's
Aid Society, which guaranteed to provide my nestling with loving, compassionate parents—who would not, by the way, be
creeps, criminals, or slutty teenage losers.

At first, I felt good about my decision. It would soon be over.
No deposit, no return. I would give birth and go away. Maybe I
would have a new room. Maybe I could get a new boyfriend.
Maybe I would go to Spain. Maybe I would become a ceramicist,
a masseuse, or a tree hugger. Maybe I would find a job, write a
book, save the world, meet a rock star, get kidnapped by aliens.
Case closed. Door shut. Night-night.

Every evening after lights out, Ramona and I would lie in our
little pink beds and plan the rest of our lives: Ramona would take
her infant son back to Pico Rivera, where her mom, dad, stepmother,
stepfather, brothers, sisters, cousins, stepbrothers, stepsisters, and
stepcousins waited to help her baptize and babysit him. In her
extended clan, she could be assured of at least one relative to help
her get a job, dry the dishes, buy a car, score some dope, or break
the thighbones of her faithless, shit-heel ex-boyfriend Ramón,

who, in keeping with Florence Crittenton policy, had betrayed Ramona with a no good *puta*-whore the moment she was two miles from her house.

My family, meanwhile, had made my position clear: I would give my baby away and return home to lie in a field of puce. My belly would deflate and my breasts would droop. Every glance from my parents would reveal their burden; every interaction, their shame. I would keep to myself because I deserved myself. I would show no sorrow because I deserved no sorrow. I would show no joy because I deserved no joy. I would be very, very quiet so as not to further disturb the lives I had already besmirched.

My path was marked.

Until one December twilight when I awoke wide-eyed and wailing in my tormented little bed, seized by a vision of Christmases Yet to Come. It was 5:00 a.m. as I waddled down the corridors of time, allowing the future to bullet out before me in endless Polaroids of pain:

I would return home.

I would return to school.

Friends would point.

Strangers would whisper.

Neighbors would snuffle into their Sunday gloves.

Everyone would know where I had been, but no one would mention it. People would be careful and look concerned, but soon they would all forget. My parents. My friends. The Weasel. No one but me would ever really remember that I was there, in that bed, my hands on that heartbeat.

The years would go by, and I would walk through malls and look at faces. I would trawl amusement parks for familiar gestures. I would search the feet of children on the beach to see if their second toe listed to the left, like mine. I would wonder every day. I would worry every night.

And no one would feel sorry for me but me.

Okay, I said to myself. For now, I'll keep my mouth shut. I'll toe the line. But when the time comes, I'm going to keep my baby.

My parents, my friends, my adoption workers, and a hastily assembled team of prepaid psychologists would not be able to talk me out of keeping my child. They would tell me I was crazy, that I was making a terrible mistake, that my life didn't have to be determined by an accident. But I would know better: you can make all the plans you want, but accidents are the plans that are made for you.

When destiny calls, I say, pick up the phone.

10

We'll Be Together

accidentally started my own coproduction company back in 1985, thanks to a faux-blond male hairdresser wearing a navy blue sailor suit, who decided to take $2,000 out of my Limelight petty cash envelope in order to procure illegal stimulants for an eighties anthem band named after Dorothy's dog in a famous children's film, and then didn't give me a receipt.

I guess I should've known that Giorgio wasn't being paid a thousand dollars a day for his grooming skills, since he didn't know how to operate a dryer, use scissors, or employ a brush. On the other hand, he did demonstrate an uncommon flair for random, frenetic hair ratting, which became obvious only after the eight-year-old actors who were portraying 1950s English farm lads showed up on set with five-inch Brigitte Bardot bubble-dos.

I still didn't understand the precise nature of Giorgio's *real* services until one of the band members invited me into his dressing room to order veggie sushi, complain about the sugared soft drinks, and mention that he had recently been saved by the Lord from the cravings of hard-drug addiction while he was in the middle of snorting a big, fat line of fine white powder.

"Er, aren't you actually doing hard drugs right now?" I asked, confused. After all, the new band member had been brought in to replace the old band member, who was rumored to have been placed in an undisclosed facility for two or three decades of involuntary rehabilitation.

"Cocaine has been proven by medical science to be completely nonaddictive, even if you do it every day, praise Jesus!" said the singer, proving that you can be a deeply devout person who is still a badly coiffed nose tweaker. "Now, please give Giorgio two thousand dollars to go and run an important, er, music video–related errand for me."

"No way." I stood fast.

I had absolutely no intention of enabling an alleged narcotics transaction on the part of a style poseur who wanted me to give up my precious production company money to some skeeze with a mullet. Due to an early teen trauma involving a Manhattan Beach Frye boot salesman with offensive body odor and superfluous facial hair, I had strong negative feelings about the pompatus of love. Besides, I might really need that money later, for foamcore, afternoon tea treats, or some extra packs of cigarettes for the grip, lighting, and production teams.

Then somebody threatened to shut down the production and pull out all my battery cables, so the record company told me that I had to allow the hairdresser to "have access to" my production assistants, so they could drive all over the hinterlands of Los Angeles in order to secure several thousand dollars worth of undocumented "beauty supplies."

"Fine," I said. "Be that way."

Life proceeded apace until the following week, when I was called on the financial carpet by the Limelight production accountant, who refused to approve my final paycheck just because my completed petty cash envelope had nothing in it except for an eight-by-ten-inch piece of notebook paper that said "TWO THOUSAND DOLLARS FOR STUPID COCAINE FOR THE STUPID BAND."

"You should know better, Sharon! We're going to take this

money out of your check if you can't produce an official receipt from an approved vendor."

As the drug dealers in Compton tended to produce vendor receipts in the form of amputated limb stumps, I finally had to threaten to sue Limelight to get my producer's fee, causing the company to become annoyed with me, causing them to stop calling me for the rock video work I had become desperately reliant upon. Because now that I was bringing home an income, my family had started to get used to hot water and electricity, not to mention the Atari hardware I had promised my son so that he could flunk out of the sixth grade and get grounded until a comet destroyed earth.

Maybe, I thought to myself, it was time for me to stop taking shit and start giving it to others instead!

"Hey, everybody!" I went around telling, er, everybody, "I'm going to start my own music video production company and make myself a truckload of music video money!"

"Har-har-har!" everybody told me back. "You can't make a crapload of money doing rock videos! You do the rock videos to build up the commercial reels, then you use the commercial reels to fund the independent features, then you use the independent features to get noticed, so you can sell your company to a multinational software-and-media corporation right before they figure out that you never made any money doing rock videos in the first place!"

"Du-uh," I replied, secretly horrified.

Because even though I'd once considered holding the spunk towel on a low-budget, nonunion porn film, I'd never thought twice about working on—ewww, ick!—commercials. Like all decent Americans, I'd spent a good part of my life hunting for the television remote so I could avoid them instead. To a socialistically inclined ex–hippie chick with a paternal Aunt Ruthie who was once the managing editor of the New York *Daily Worker*, the prospect of foisting douche and detergents onto unsuspecting consumers was only slightly less odious than eating stink beetles.

What I needed was a partner! Then maybe I could make *him* do all the commercials. Besides, I was afraid to go it alone. As a gutless, whimpering codependent with a deep-seated fear of personal accountability, I have always depended on the kindness of others, especially when it comes to the dreary details of structure, reliability, and discipline.

After putting out the word that I was in the cohort market, I finally got introduced to "the Partner" by the video commissioner of Warner Bros. Records, who had steadfastly refused to quit her prestigious, high-paying job in order to form a struggling partnership with me. In an annoying video postscript, this very same executive went on to attain good health, exalted status, and great big bags of cold hard cash when she achieved every American's dream of being bought out of her contract in a massive corporate reshuffle.

What follows represents a blow-by-blow account of the birth and death of my first company, NO Pictures.

GROUND ZERO, EARLY SUMMER 1985

The Partner and I have our first lunch meeting at a hot Italian bistro on trendy Melrose Avenue, in the heart of East Hollywood. This is where I feed my very own personal family at least nine meals a week. The food is good, the price is right, and if you want to be cool, you have to eat cool. Besides, Angeli is the only restaurant that delivers to my gut-green and white Fairfax apartment, where I live next door to prefamous George Clooney, a punk band called the Fibonaccis, two soon-to-be-famous Swiss artists, and three thousand hairy and extremely procreative Orthodox Jews who wear wide-brimmed beaver hats in the middle of July.

Meanwhile, the Partner and I try to discuss business while knocking back panini, Pollo Arrosto, tiramisu, biscotti, snickerdoodles, cappuccinos, double espressos, and two hundred packs of nonlite filtered cigarettes. Then I realize that I'm feeling edgy, antsy, and ill at ease.

I'm pretty sure it isn't from the indigestible animal fats, the buckets of Italian plain roast, or the rapidly inhaled bronchial carcinogens that we're still allowed to pollute the unventilated room with because huge public litigation suits have not been invented yet.

No, I believe that I'm feeling edgy, antsy, and ill at ease because the Partner appears to hate me. On the plus side, he is tall, good-looking, well built, intelligent, and well shod, with an impressive résumé, expensive clothes, and a super-long list of groovy celebrity ex-girlfriends. On the other hand, he is the eighties version of a Hollywood rat packer—cool, poised, slick, charmingly caddish, fast with a smile, and slow to pick up the check.

Which is probably why nothing I say, do, wear, think, am, are, or ever intend to be will ever meet with even a modicum of his modest approval and vice versa. He's not my type and I'm not his, which might explain why he ignores my questions, discounts my experience, dodges my inquiries, evades my scrutiny, and sneers at my ideas. On the other hand, he sweet-talks all the cute waitresses, most of the cute customers, and a couple of cute busgirls.

Once again I realize that men only pretend to like you when they want to fuck you, which only becomes obvious when they don't want to fuck you, because then they don't bother to pretend. Naturally, this offends every part of me that is poised to believe that a woman is something more than a vagina on legs. On the other hand, I'm hurt when someone does not approve of my vagina or legs.

Uh-oh. The Partner is everything that is bad for me.

On the other hand, he says he can raise the other $2,500 we need to get an office and some stationery.

Oh well. He is the only person I have ever met who smokes more than I do. That takes commitment.

The Partner and I agree to start the Company.

Well, actually, I agree to start the Company, and the Partner doesn't say no.

Afterward I notice that he never actually says yes either. This turns out to be a common theme in my relationships with remote, passive-aggressive men, but I don't find that out until *after* I've been in therapy for more than fifteen years, because after all, my brilliant but unconventional Dutch postcognitive psychotherapist, Dr. Hannah S. Brinker, does not get paid two hundred dollars an hour just to tell me right away how fucked up I am.

MIDSUMMER 1985

Since the Partner and I are really in business now, we toss around names for the Company. I want to do something that suggests bigness, like Universal or Paramount, but all I can think of is Really, Really, Big Pictures. Meanwhile, the Partner thinks it should be something "cool," but all he can think of is Really, Really Cool Productions. Finally, we resort to our last initials, which limits our possibilities to either ON Pictures or NO Pictures.

After a brief discussion on why it is good to be bad and when it is appropriate to be inappropriate, the Partner insists that the Company be named NO Pictures because it is a great name with strong negative-positive association. Also, he feels that it would be unmanly to let my initial go first. For reasons apparent only to Dr. Brinker, I don't see this as a red flag.

Besides, I'm distracted by the marketing campaign, which we decide will be Polaroids of famous rock stars covering their faces in mock horror as we approach to snap their pictures. For some reason, we never get around to the ads, probably because famous rock stars are always covering their faces in real horror when we approach to snap their pictures.

As we discuss the way the company will function, I talk a lot about "division of labor" while the Partner talks a lot about "keeping up appearances." I don't realize until later that when the Partner says "keeping up appearances," he means that I should dress better, and the Partner doesn't realize that when I say "division of labor," I mean he should be doing all the commercials for our soon-to-be-nonexistent advertising division.

Because shortly after being presented to me as "the commercial guy," the Partner tells me that he is more of "the noncommercial guy," because he hates "appearances," even though in *my* case he would like them to be a lot better. On the other hand, he claims we are starting our company on an equal basis, because I will come to the party with *my* hot director, Mary Lambert, and he will attend the gala with *his* smoking talent, whom we shall refer to for the purposes of this narrative as Napoleon Bonaparte.

At first, it looks like we'll be making big, fat pails of fine American samolies. Then Napoleon's manager calls to tell us that he will not allow Napoleon to work with our company, because Napoleon has "problems" and our company could be a "bad influence." I ask the Partner what he means, and the Partner says Napoleon's manager is crazy. Later we find out Napoleon is in rehab. We later find out that so is the manager. The Partner claims that he doesn't have any idea what his influence has to do with any of it.

Meanwhile, we need some more directors, because Mary is still in the south of France, prepping a stinky-cheese movie with Prince until the end of the year. Luckily, there's always the potential for "creative differences," which would mean that she could do all the work, so that Prince could get all the glory, so that she could be paid off to quit the movie, leave town, and never tell anybody what she thought about Prince.

Ho hum. I wonder what will happen?

EARLY AUGUST 1985

Now that we have a name, we decide to move out of Angeli and into a four-hundred-square-foot office that used to be a cheap, tacky fleabag motel. It's small, boxy, and has low-pile carpet that looks like a dead lawn recently scattered with cockroach skeletons. On the other hand, it has a clean bathroom.

We take it.

We get some stationery at Kinko's. My dad donates four desks, some filing cabinets, and a hideous fake-walnut conference table with chairs. We get the Sparkletts water thingie and a coffee service and a stapler and a hole punch.

We're in business.

If you view our office as a cheap, tacky fleabag motel-suite, the Partner and I have our "executive" desks arrayed back to back in the tacky living room, while our receptionist is set up in the fleabag dining room. In the entryway, we have two supplemental chairs for potential visitors, one supplemental desk for potential employees, and a free calendar because it is the only wall art we can afford. The back bedroom is our conference space, which boasts a crappy table, six chairs, and a closet where we put our stationery. Every employee receives a complimentary cheap ashtray, an inexpensive plastic in-box, and a high-class rented IBM typewriter, because we are total techno-tards and have not heard about Macintosh computers yet. We use pencils instead.

I call the old Limelight C.P.A., who helps us to form a legal corporation, set up a D.B.A., and organize a limited partnership. Then his company fires him and he goes to the Betty Ford Clinic for addiction to "rock." This is the first time I have ever heard of "rock," and the third time this year that I have heard the term "rehab," which I initially misheard to be the term "prefab."

I set the Partner up on a blind double date with me and Bill and my best friend. We all go out to dinner and the Partner drinks a bottle of Scotch, compulsively talking about himself while completely ignoring her while overtly getting the phone number of the barmaid. She (my best friend) goes home crying. He asks me the next day if I think she likes him.

I'm so confused.

LATE AUGUST 1985

The Partner and I divvy up our contacts at the record companies. Basically he knows all the women, and I know all the men. I guess that's fair.

I call Jeff Ayeroff, vice president of creative affairs at Warner Bros., and tell him that we have a new company, and that we are desperate for work and will therefore provide top-notch goods and services super fast and über cheap. He immediately tells me to go find a director for the next Chris Isaak video, "Gone Ridin,' " which will come with a $35,000 budget.

Mary is *still* in France, so her manager, Gary Kurfirst, talks us into hiring a pothead who did a Talking Heads video in which the band sings about babies while jumping up and down on bungee cables. He is willing to work for 5 percent of the gross, so he gets the gig.

Meanwhile, because "Ridin' " is a soundtrack promotion for a super-stupid movie called "American Flyer," we will be required to feature their super-stupid film footage in 50 percent of the finished video. Accordingly, we are forced to attend an advance screening, where we get to watch Kevin Costner star as the big hotshot über-athletic cocky doctor who is compelled by brotherly love to compete against his much smaller unemployed loser sibling in a three-week uphill bicycle race across the Rocky Mountains. In the feel-good ending, the successful big brother gets leukemia and dies on the side of the road.

We are sent with Chris to watch the movie at a plush private theater at Warner Bros., and the movie is so boring that we turn off the sound so we can make up alternative dialogue. Chris ends up doing all the extra voices, whom he portrays as innocent Hollywood victims looking for a bicycle path to get out of this shitty movie. In the end, he has Costner fake a cerebral hemorrhage so he can go do *Field of Dreams*.

Afterward we get to Jeff's office and I make the big mistake of bragging that I am so cool and so groovy and so down with it that I could never have made such a dreary, incoherent movie. Jeff immediately dials the head of the studio.

"Our video producer has something to tell you," he says.

"Errr," I find myself stammering. "I guess you've got a hit on your hands!"

"You mean you've got shit on your hands!" Jeff screams into the speakerphone.

Although we finish our very first NO Pictures video on time and on budget, it is a piece of poop. Jeff is annoyed and possibly getting close to getting bored with me. I promise him a makeup video, anytime, anywhere. Meanwhile, I scour the planet for more decent video directors and get on the Partner's case to come in with his much-promised director contribution. He comes up with a guy who gets a Mr. Mister video that has something to do with hair products.

Dear God, please make Mary have creative differences and come home from France.

SEPTEMBER 1985

The Partner and I are having "differences."

We both put in an "eight-hour day," except that I come into the office at 8:00 a.m. and leave at 6:00, and he comes in at 6:00 p.m. and leaves at 11:00. He won't let the employees go home until he does, and when I ask them what he is doing, they say he is sitting at his desk while he talks on the phone and scribbles his name over and over on the desk pad. He goes out every night. I go home every night. He has ninety-seven girlfriends. I have one dude.

The only thing we have in common is an overwhelming fear of failure. The Partner deals with his fear through palliative measures. I deal with mine through bitching and moaning. Guess who wins? No one.

Meanwhile, the Partner—who steadfastly denies having any associations with any of the women who keep calling and claiming to be his girlfriend—has a bad habit of forging new assignations before ending the old ones by purposely leaving around a suggestive photo of somebody who isn't the person who finds it. The reason I know this is because they all keep calling me to ask who the chick in the picture is. Luckily, I know nothing. The Partner keeps his secrets close, unlike his Polaroids.

OCTOBER 1985

Jeff invites the director Lyndall Hobbs and me to a "listening party" at Warner Bros. for Paul Jabara, who starred on Broadway in *Hair* and *The Rocky Horror Show* and *Jesus Christ Superstar*. He also wrote the song "It's Raining Men."

Unfortunately, Paul's career is now as dead as disco, and he's trying to revive it with a nine-and-a-half-minute disco "popcretta" about an unhappy housewife who finds true love and real meaning in a relationship with a seven-foot-tall black man who has a twelve-inch rocket in his pocket.

I'm not kidding.

The place is packed with rich, long-haired ex-hippie record company executives who look like they might not be that comfortable being sandwiched in a small room with a guy who's entirely comfortable miming fellatio on himself while he prances, bobs, and kicks like a deranged Rockette on the top of the Warner Bros. conference table for nine minutes.

Then he's done. There is a breathless silence.

Jeff sighs.

"This will be the best video in the history of the world," he says. "Or the worst."

He's right.

Meanwhile, Paul has recorded the song "Ocho Rios" with Pat Ast, who is a three-hundred-pound Halston runway model and Warhol Superstar. She's also as scary as a sharp ax in a dark alley. Paul's no withering violet himself, and the two of them have spent

years honing the most volatile, offensive, explosive codependency
I've ever witnessed. In our preproduction meetings they're constantly screaming obscenities and hurling sharp objects at each
other, especially if there are any new witnesses around. They particularly delight in horrifying strangers.

"Fat, stupid, hideous, talentless cunt!" Paul will address his
muse on a good day.

"Fucking faggot pig fucker!" Pat will return in kind, right before they fall into each other's arms and start giggling like little
girls at a pony show.

Then, on the first day of shooting, Paul reveals to Pat that owing
to popular demand (his), Paul is now playing Pat's part, in drag.

"But don't worry," he explains gleefully, handing her the new
script, "you still have a very significant leading role . . . as the Fat,
Ugly Record Company Secretary Who Can't Ever Get Laid!"

Exploding with sadistic glee, Paul bursts out with a titter that
sounds exactly like Tweety Bird on helium. Then, as the entire
crew watches in horror, Pat grabs Paul's head and starts twisting
it like the screw top on a beer bottle.

"You treacherous, butt-fucking, sybaritic cow cocksucker!"
Pat screams.

Paul's ear is bleeding and his false eyelashes are frightfully askew
by the time the grip team pulls Pat off of him. Then Pat is driven
home by our thirty-five-year-old production assistant, who helps
her into her house after she fakes a fainting attack. Then Pat locks
all the doors and windows and holds him hostage.

"Sharon, you have to help me!" Johnny pleads by phone twenty
minutes later. "Pat is very upset and she won't release me until
Paul pays her five hundred dollars!" The check is cut, Johnny is
released, and Pat shows up for work the next day as if nothing had
ever happened.

Meanwhile, Lyndall works her ass off, Paul drives everyone
insane, and the video is my nominee for the most impertinent
material ever made. Paul and Pat are gone now, lost to AIDS and

diabetes, but I heard that the video went on to become a big hit in some of the less discriminating gay clubs. I also heard that Paul got beat up in the bar of the Pierre Hotel, after he bribed the concierge to put it on the in-house television system in the false hope that Liza Minnelli would wander in and see it.

NOVEMBER 1985

Things are getting worse with the Partner.

I pretty much never see him now, at least not if he sees me first.

Every day I make a vow to make our relationship better and every day it gets way worse. I don't know why. I try to be nice to him, but that only makes him suspicious. I scare him. I horrify him. I fill him with fear, loathing, and resentment.

Ho hum. Walk it off, dude.

Meanwhile, I take the opportunity to convince my boyfriend, Bill, that he should quit his new job as a city defense attorney in order to become a rock video cinematographer. Hey, he only went to college for twelve years and passed the bar while going to night school while working as a law clerk and being a father and the domestic partner of a flat-broke future producer with two cats.

Is that really as important as hanging out with Hüsker Dü?

DECEMBER 1985

Annette Cirillo, who is one of the Partner's female record company contacts, hires us to do a video for a heavy metal band called Autograph.

We go with the director to a meeting at Jerry's Famous Deli, in the hideous Valley, where the band tells us that they aren't like other bands because they are "so fucking ugly." It's true. They are so fucking ugly. They like ugly chicks too, and they want some for their video. The record company representative says no. Ugly guys must have hot girls in their videos. They argue. We compromise and end up with some of the band's ugly chicks and some of the record company's hot chicks. Interestingly, Bill feels that the record company hot chicks are way uglier than the ugly ones.

Meanwhile, the Partner caravans to the first day of shooting with my boyfriend, who notes that the Partner drives sixty-five miles per hour while remaining in second gear for 120 miles. By the time he gets to the location, the Partner's clutch is burned out and his Renault Le Car is hauled off for experimentation.

Then the Partner borrows a petty cash envelope and the record company executive's car to go to a 7-Eleven. He doesn't return for seven hours.

There is widespread panic, as everyone assumes he is dead. The production assistants check the hospitals and morgues. Then he comes back. The car has no gas. He swears he just went to a 7-Eleven. Somehow he charms the record company executive into going out to dinner and not killing him, then they both drive off into the sunset as she awards him some overages.

Because, somehow, the thing is, the Partner is the most charming man on the planet to everyone on earth but me, to whom he is the meanest, most dismissive person on the planet. It's like being in *Gaslight*.

Oh well. At least Bill loves me, almost as much as he is loved by good ol' Autograph, who think he is the greatest cinematographer on earth. As we wave goodbye, they offer him their ultimate compliment.

"Bill, you are a real fuckin' fucker."

So true.

FEBRUARY 1986

Jeff Ayeroff calls to introduce me to Matt Mahurin, a brilliant young graphic artist and still photographer who has done the inaugural album cover for a band called the BoDeans. Jeff wants me to help

Matt transmute his intriguing photographic technique from stills to motion pictures. He wants me to take him on and show him the ropes. He wants me to do so at a very reasonable rate.

I agree.

Matt comes into town and we pick him up at the airport and spend the day working with him. Matt's mysterious technique is revealed to involve lots of spit and a pencil eraser.

Bill works with Matt to figure out a film stock that will work best with spit and pencil erasers. They experiment with negatives that make the grain look like golf balls. They pull the film out of the camera and walk on it. They smear Vaseline over the lens, spray it with saline solution, and put a shower cap over it.

When the day is over, we take Matt to his complimentary room at the Hollywood Roosevelt Hotel, which has just reopened. There are huge bouquets of flowers and jumbo baskets of fruit in the lobby. Matt gets super excited and thinks we've thrown him a giant, star-studded party.

"Gee . . ." sighs Matt (he actually says stuff like "gee"), "I really like this video thing."

We don't tell him for eleven years that the party wasn't for him.

In contrast to his photography and graphic work, which is scary and brooding, Matt is open and loving. He puts his darkness in the videos, so by the time the BoDeans video is done, it looks like a bat cave inside a bat cave with a couple of vague figures toting guitars that occasionally run through the frame.

Everyone tells Matt that the video is too long, but he doesn't agree, and then everybody fights about it, and then he wins, and then it is a spectacular success. Matt becomes the go-to guy for art, vision, and earnestness. He is young, stubborn, intense, and idealistic, so we fight about everything, all the time, which makes us become best friends.

Meanwhile, I fight with the Partner all the time too, which makes us become total enemies. Life is weird.

MARCH 1986

Mary returns from France, where she has finally experienced "creative differences" with Prince, who has finally changed his job description from "rock star" to "movie star" to "director." Mary never says that he is an unprofessional lunkhead or a dick, so I assume she was paid well.

In the meantime, Mary already has another movie to direct, so we try to get a simple Madonna video shoot for "La Isla Bonita," which still ends up with three sets and four days and a downtown location shoot with five hundred people of Hispanic descent, plus two Chihuahuas. Madonna wears a full-on flamenco dress and looks fabulous, except that her breasts fall out of her gown when she does a back bend, as usual.

Sean is on the set, glowering, as usual. No one knows why.

I love Madonna. Everyone knows why.

For some reason, no one at the record company has a lyric sheet, and it sounds like the song is saying "Last night I dreamed of a bagel." Maybe Sean prefers bialys.

MAY 1986

Jeff Ayeroff introduces me to Michael Patterson and Candace Reckinger, the live action–animation duo who have done the a-ha "Take on Me" video. I love their work. Candace is a totally happening hipster and feminist. Michael is one of those animation genius types.

Rich Frankel and Jeff Gold at A&M want us to do a video for Suzanne Vega's "Luca," a song about violent child abuse. They ask if we can make the video kinda "up." *Hmmm.* We go to New York and somehow pull it off. The video's a hit.

We get a couple of Sting videos. He's so cute.

My friend Becky has a friend named Tammy, who just got out

of film school. She's great and gung-ho, and sweet as pie, so we hire her as a director too.

Bill directs the Replacements' "The Ledge" with Randy Skinner, the video executive from Warner Bros. I don't know why it takes two directors do one single shot of a stereo speaker, but it stays near the top of the list of Greatest Videos of All Time for twenty years, which for MTV is apparently eternity.

JULY 1986

Bill and I go to New York to shoot a video for Kitaro with Matt Mahurin. Kitaro is the top-selling artist in Japan. He has hair down to his butt and lives on top of Mount Fuji. His music is "New Age," which means it doesn't have a tune or words that rhyme.

"He's the Madonna of Japan!" his manager tells us. Interestingly, this is what every single manager of every single artist I've ever worked with from Japan *always* says.

On a whim Bill and I decide to get married, so the Morgans Hotel, where we are staying, gives us the penthouse free for a week. We get wedding rings at the flea market across the street.

Note: Mine broke while I was cracking an egg four years later.

Meanwhile, I go to Bendel's to look for a wedding dress, and the salesperson sneers derisively when I say that I am getting married that weekend.

"*Hah!* Honey, we have customers who come to us for a fitting two years before the wedding."

I try on a sizing model that fits perfectly the first time. *Hah* back at ya, honey. Then I discover that it costs more than six months' rent plus all the accompanying overhead at my two-bedroom West Hollywood Fairfax District apartment. The sales chick is still scoffing at me, so I buy it anyway.

We call all the relatives on Thursday and have the ceremony

on Saturday. Matt hires a master cellist. Our clergyperson works for the United Nations, so he gives us a Presbyterian-Buddhist-Shiite ceremony and then we smash the glass, mazel tov style. Everybody eats chicken and gets drunk. Kitaro gives us the first CD player ever made.

The Partner comes to the wedding. Even though he's never been hitched, he is super sentimental about eternal love. I guess we're getting along, because he's smiling with all my relatives in every one of my wedding pictures.

"That 'partner guy' is great!" Jim Bennett, my new father-in-law, toasts our wedding. "You should have married him!"

We stay in the penthouse for two weeks until Mary's manager puts Joe Strummer, formerly of the Clash, in there on my recommendation. He totally trashes the place in ten minutes. The Morgans management never offers me a good deal again.

AUGUST 1987

It's one year later, and NO Pictures is fabulously successful. We're doing lots of videos and getting lots of directors, and everything is going really well, if you don't count the fact that I'm attending two postcognitive psychotherapeutic sessions per week in order to deal with my deteriorating relationship with the Partner, who has recently taken to calling me at home, late at night, to call me names and accuse me of crimes. Then, the next day, he denies calling and says I am crazy. I tell him he is on drugs.

He repeats that I am crazy.

Only once before have I engaged in a relationship that was so fraught with hostility, tension, competition, and aggression.

Omigod. My partner is my mother.

So I confront the Partner.

I say that he's irrational, paranoid, cruel, and "having a problem" with drugs.

He says I'm crazy, psycho, and "having a problem" with being a ball-busting bitch.

I tell him that if he agrees to go to rehab, I'll totally support him. Otherwise we should break up.

He tells me he's going to think about it.

AUGUST 1987, LATER THAT NIGHT

The Partner calls me and tells me he doesn't have "a problem." Furthermore, he insists that I'm an aggressive, competitive psycho-bitch and that all of his friends and some of his relatives agree that I'm definitely out to bust his balls.

"Big wow," I say, "you still 'have a problem.'"

He says "the problem" is me.

We agree to disagree by agreeing to break up.

We both take our initials and start new companies. We are both very successful. Mine is called "O Pictures." His is still going.

Postscript: It occurs to me that I might have been the only adult in my end of the entertainment community who was not on nonprescription mood-altering drugs for 80 percent of every day in the mid-eighties, which makes me feel sad and glad and mad at exactly the same time.

Papa Don't Preach

At 3:55 a.m. on January 5, 1972, following a compulsory enema, the enforced shaving of my pubic thatch, and an all-night infusion of industrial-strength Demerol, a ten-pound infant was extracted from my womb with twenty-four-inch stainless steel surgical tongs.

I was sixteen years old when I gave birth alone.

My body was cleaved, my spirit ravaged, and my heart made ash.

But that was nothing compared to the desolation of the dawn. Walls stained, legs splayed, jaw slack, I watched as I was ripped and rethreaded. Meanwhile, my son was whisked efficiently from the room.

They did not bother to show me his face.

"Give him b-ba-a-ack!" I screeched.

"Stop that caterwauling!" Dr. Black, the on-duty obstetrician, scolded, glowering at my vagina as if it were loitering on a street corner, panhandling for change. "And don't move! I'm still working here!"

Dr. Black had spent the entire evening cheerfully dicing up my happy bits, but now that it was time to stitch the whole thing back together, he was in a really bad mood.

Me too.

"Give me back my fucking baby, you whore!" I howled. Like

all the women of my clan, I am compelled under the slightest duress to swear like a filthy, disgusting sailor.

"Forget it!" barked Black. "Girls who might give their babies up for adoption don't get to see their babies because they are psychologically unstable and a bad influence on young people. Besides, they won't want to give them back. Now hush your filthy mouth so I can finish here!"

Dr. Black did not appear too busy to hijack my baby. Moreover, he seemed inclined to jam a stick of dynamite up my ass and light the fuse. Luckily, my slumbering Jewess awoke to steer the proceedings toward a more favorable conclusion.

"I said, give me my baby . . . or . . . I'll fucking sue!"

With visions of my thundering Semitic vengeance stampeding across his capacious vacation home in Aspen, Dr. Black dropped his scalpel, surrendered his sponges, and heaved a deep and painful sigh.

"Ohhhh. Okay. As you wish."

And so the nurse was instructed to hand my baby boy to me. At last, at last.

"Great Caesar's ghost!" she enthused as she lugged him across the room like a sack of cats.

Note: I have never heard this phrase before or since, except on *Superman* television reruns.

"This is the biggest illegitimate white infant I have ever seen!" she exclaimed.

Luckily, no one knew in those days about the effects of secondhand smoke on embryos, so there were none. Despite solid scientific evidence now linking nicotine exposure to very low birth weights, my son had swelled to a majestic nine pounds, eleven ounces by his delivery date. I attribute this scientific miracle to my very committed policy of eating even more than I smoked.

"Why, thank you . . ." I fluttered. At every low point in life, it's advisable to take credit for *something*, even if that something is how fat and white your recently delivered bastard is.

"Hmmmph," sulked the doctor, irate that I was getting attention that didn't involve inflamed tissue coming into contact with a sharp object. "You are a very rash young girl, and you will be very, very, sorry."

Tucked into my arms, head soft as squid, eyes like bright blue arrows, my big baby looked at me, and I looked back.

I was *not* sorry.

"I'm really keeping him . . ." I slurred dreamily, whiffing at his head. "What does it eat anyhow?"

Without waiting for a reply, I nodded off for thirty-six straight hours, after which my parents came by to jump-start a strict postnatal regimen of eternal castigation. To their horror, instead of flogging myself with a rotted umbilical cord, they found me sitting on my hospital cot with a cheery Korean postpartum nurse, trilling a *Bye Bye, Birdie* medley to my brand-new baby boy.

"No, no, stop! You will not keep it!" my mother screamed. "Do you hear me? Give that child back this instant!"

"You can't make me!" I squeaked possessively. "I've got rights!"

"Rights, schmights!" reprimanded my father. "You can't bring that baby home! We told Grandma Rose you were at Passover camp!"

"Oh yeah? Well, fuck Grandma Rose!"

A hush fell over the room. My parents had been through three wars, two kids, and the Great Depression, but enough was enough! *Nobody* fucks Grandma Rose!

It was time to deliver the parental edict: on the advice of their therapist, their therapist's therapist, and somebody they knew whom this had happened to at Temple Beth Ohr, I was never to darken their doorstep again.

"As long as you choose this course of action, you are completely on your own," my father announced.

"Yeah. Call us when you give up," my mother encouraged.

"Boo-hoo-hoo!" I replied, initiating a crying jag that would last most of the next four and a half months. My desperate situation struck me as hilarious and surreal, but only for the thirty out of every sixty seconds that it didn't leave me feeling hysterical and bereft. Fortunately, the more mentally unbalanced I became, the more my four-hundred-pound Korean postpartum attendant wanted to fix me up. As far as she was concerned, it was her calling to make me happy and I was getting in the way.

"You leave now, goddammit!" Nurse Soo thundered at my reddening parents, smacking them toward the exit with her large ungainly palms. "You upset patient! You goddamn bad!"

"Hey! You can't hit me!" protested my mother, raising her hands to defend herself.

"I no damn hit!" Nurse Soo lied, simultaneously delivering a sound slap to the back of my mom's skull. "You out! Hospital rules!" she continued to fib, allowing the door to firmly strike my father on his ass.

"Yeah! Er, take that!" I said, supporting her confusedly, until Nurse Soo whipped around and unleashed her grammar on me.

"You stop cying! You look baby! You happy!" Nurse Soo screeched, gesticulating wildly.

"Yes ma'am," I replied.

And so I stopped crying, looked at my baby, and got happy. Minute by minute, my heart was fractured, made whole, and then rebroken. The only way to survive was to surrender my pain to a higher authority, even if she was a morbidly obese gynecological nurse.

It was obvious that I needed to make alternative housing arrangements, so I decided to call my alternative best friend, Martha Babbe, queen of the loose-hipped vegan chicks. Martha played the finger cymbals, had not eaten animal flesh since junior high, and was so liberated that she didn't even wear underpants under her madras miniskirt. Unfortunately, she was usually busy getting incarcerated against her will.

"Hey, Marth, I just had my baby, and my parents kicked me

out, and I have no money and no place to live. So can I move in with you, like, next Thursday?"

"Oh man, that would be soooo fine . . ." she replied. "But my parents are having me committed to Gateway Mental Hospital again, just because I sold their car and gave the money to that kundalini sex guy at that ashram that got closed by the feds."

"Fascists!" I replied indignantly. It was so typical of parents to think more about a Mercedes than about tantric yoga.

Disappointed, I moved on to best friend number two, revered by the community for her ability to take more psilocybin than God. Suzanne Mayau and I had been through a lot together, including getting expelled from Mr. Nunn's typing class, learning to play Stratego on peyote buttons, and memorizing all the lyrics to Grand Funk Railroad. She was funny, she had her own Chevy Super Sport, and she owned a horse and a goat who practiced interspecies love. More important, her grandpa was a Lithuanian "union" boss who worked the San Pedro harbor, so she always got free shellfish.

"Hey, Leadfoot!" I greeted Suzanne, who had the body of Raquel Welch and the boots of John Denver. "Wanna get a place together and raise a baby with me? We could make bouillabaisse."

"Sorry, man," said Suzanne. "I got busted last weekend on fifteen hits of Sunshine, because I was trying to bite Johnny Winters's leg at the San Bernardino Swing Auditorium. I'm grounded for, like, ever, man!"

Bummer.

Now that I was a high school sophomore with no parents, no job, and a ten-pound screaming infant, all I needed was a home, some money, and someone to tell me what a baby did.

I was inexperienced, immature, and stupid as a bucket of paint. I had never taken care of anyone or anything, and nobody had ever shown me how. I didn't own baby clothes, diapers, rubber pants, a crib, toys, food, or a bottle kit. I didn't have a car, a house, a bank account, or a husband. I had never earned money, written a check, cleaned a house, driven a car, or done my own laundry.

Since I didn't know anything or anybody who did, I decided to just do nothing and let the universe work around me. Common knowledge in the seventies suggested that if you could just let it be, then you could be here now, and that would be . . . um . . . good? In the meantime, to facilitate my lack of house, apartment, or tenement slum, Nurse Soo fiddled with my medical charts to extend my hospital stay.

"You very sick! Hah hah hah! I give you horriblest infection! Hah hah hah! You stay one month, no problem! Hah hah hah!"

Nurse Soo had a plan that I make a real plan, real soon. In the meantime, I would watch TV, read magazines, and smoke six cartons of Virginia Slims per week. Now that there were no adults to monitor me, my habit had gone from mild to monkey-size.

Three weeks passed before I made a move that didn't involve lifting a long ecru cigarette to my lips. Every three hours they would bring my baby in for me to cuddle and bottle-feed, as Dr. Black had taken it upon himself to inject me with a secret hormone formula that dried up all the milk in my breasts. On the plus side, I lost sixty pounds in ten days.

As the clock ticked and I contemplated being cast out into the night, the very hairy legs of Dr. Leah Weissman, the hippie psychiatric social worker who had recently incited the sensitivity riots at the Florence Crittenton Home, came galumphing through my brain. Although Dr. Leah had lost her job, I had kept her phone number. She contacted a prominent foster care agency and helped me place my son into a temporary home so I could get out of the hospital without losing custody. Then I went to a lawyer to qualify myself for "emancipated minor status," a legal ruse that allowed me to achieve premature adulthood so I could sign a lease, go on welfare, and receive food stamps. Now I could go bankrupt, go to federal prison, and lease my own tenement, just like everybody else in America!

Although we swore to remain friends forever, after Ramona Remedios and I left Florence Crittenton for our respective homes with our respective babies, I talked to her only a couple of times by phone. She claimed she was doing great, mostly because her favorite stepcousin had finally kicked the shit out of her faithless, shit-heel ex-boyfriend Ramón, with whom she had already gotten back together and broken up six or seven times. They are probably still getting married and divorced, for all I know.

Rooster gave her baby up for adoption after dropping it on the hospital floor. Felicia got pregnant by her forty-year-old married black boyfriend and finally got to be a maternity resident.

I haven't been back since I left those many years ago, but according to Google, the Florence Crittenton Center of Los Angeles, founded in 1892, still provides residential treatment services for abused and neglected adolescent girls, teen mothers, and their infants. There are still plenty of them to go around.

(Sorta) Like a Prayer

t's four in the morning, December 12, 1988, and Madonna pumps to the beat, swinging her hips and syncing her lips with the kind of grim, methodical rhythm that does not alter and will not falter until the second line of the fourth chorus of the "dance against racism burning-cross spiritually indicative yet overtly sexual Watusi" sequence when she accidentally grinds her bare left instep into a mini saguaro cactus.

I gasp.

She doesn't.

A flinty ex-Catholic who was tutored from an early age on how to take an impalement like a man, Madonna gets right back on the job, hop-stepping and cool-jerking until the very last note of the "extended house eternal disco fadeout," when she finally slumps to her oozing feet with a muffled whimper, a bold "Keeeeriiistt!" and something that sounds exactly like "Fuck-meeeejeesszus!"

Because it's "Just like a prayer . . ."

Amen, sister.

We're filthy, we're freezing, and we've got six-foot crosses blazing all around us like Titan missiles—you can smell the smoke all the way to Compton.

But that's not all you can smell. Just to the south of the un-cultivated hillside of the abandoned air force base in San Pedro, behind the flotilla of reeking chemical toilets-on-wheels, the picked-over remains of yesterday's craft service, and the brown-on-brown, diesel-leaking production Winnebago where several low-level production assistants are hiding so they'll be able to take a nap out of walkie-talkie range, I can see a long line of law enforcement vehicles wending their way onto base with their lights flashing.

"Shits on toast!" Hildy, my producer, approaches me. "The po-lice keep coming. Something about civil rights and an enhanced penalty for hate crime?"

I sigh. Obviously, the local population has ignored the mim-eographed BURNING CROSS shooting announcements that we carefully stapled to every other telephone pole so that they wouldn't alert the local chapter of the NAACP before barricading themselves down in their basements to prepare for the Ku Klux Klan invasion that's obviously to come.

"We're innocent, officer. Think about it: What kind of crazed racial hater ever had this kind of budget?" I appeal to a deeply aggravated police lieutenant fifteen minutes later, pointing out the skilled team of pyrotechnicians who had to dig out fuel lines for two weeks to provide direct feeds to these hi-tech babies, which are constructed of asbestos, wired for sound, and equipped with enough petroleum product to get us all to hell and back. "I can absolutely (pretty much) assure you that we're one-hundred percent (or very nearly) legally location permitted for three hun-dred people, two hundred vehicles, and twenty diesel-fueled flaming crucifixes!"

The fog's rolling in, we've been shooting for nineteen hours, and dawn's starting to crack, but we've gotta get the COAF (Cover-Our-Ass Footage) just in case MTV goes pussy and refuses to air, say, the extreme close-ups of ketchup and Hershey's syrup that'll be splurting out of Madonna's prosthetic palm stigmata (second choral bridge, stanza five), or the "miracle transubstantiation un-natural lovemaking" sequence (lines six through ten, stanza two), in which our heroine dry-humps a black paper-mâché church icon (in order to stamp out human rights abuse).

Then my director, Mary Lambert, yells "Cut!" and Madonna starts to look *just* like somebody who's done the Hokey Pokey for five and a half minutes on top of a ripe succulent. So immediately our crew starts to mutter and moan and stampede like crazed bison at a prairie fire, muttering obscenities and elbowing one another in the ribs as they scramble to get to Madonna first so they can powder her nose, adjust her straps, plump her ringlets, pluck her brows, tamp her cuticles, knead her shoulders, feed her face, and salve her wounds.

"Bactine, bandages, and back to fucking one!" screeches the assistant director, but, blah, blah, nobody pays attention to him. In our world, Madonna is not just the Real Thing, she's the Only Thing, the preeminent, postmodern, MTV über chick who can drop and do fifty with the *Oxford English Dictionary* strapped to her ankles while talking dirty, crocheting baby blankets, and trading silver commodities in a Wonderbra.

I mean, c'mon! This is the eighties! The decade of me! Me, me, me, that's all we ever think about, unless we're thinking about Madonna. Madonna's almost as interesting as me! She's the churning, burning spirit child of our collective unconscious. She knows what we want, and she gets there first. She anticipates our secrets and acts out our needs. In the sinkhole of popular culture, she offers us the heft of a psychosexual context. In the tundra of contemporary programming, she offers us the idea of having an idea. She makes money seem serious. She makes sex look reli-gious. Most important, she makes narcissism look hot.

Which is why we've been hired to delude the American public if ever she threatens to slip in under par, to swab, tweeze, spackle, and squeeze until she is every inch the pop goddess we've cracked her up to be.

For now, our work's cut out for us. Madonna's foot looks like shredded wheat, there are bags under her eyes you could stuff with tuna cans, and her frisky left boob has once again freed itself from the skimpy restraints of her bark brown, Sophia Loren fuck-me slip.

Fuel's leaking from Crucifix Number Six, the Crow's-Feet-Obliterating Eyelight has a busted lamp, and the videotape recording unit is on the fritz. Hostile inquiries are flying in from *Ebony* magazine, rumors of a boycott are arriving from Pepsi-Cola, Warner Bros. is threatening to cancel the second payment, and somebody named Captain Bob is chasing me with a post-dated subpoena with regard to a dented anchor, a burning toilet, and a hundred-foot yachting foremast that has mysteriously gone missing following the second reshoot of Mötley Crüe's "Don't Go Away Mad (Just Go Away)."

Ho hum. Business as usual. After all, I began my professional relationship with Madonna while dressed in a clown suit.

It was 1985, on the set of the "Material Girl" video, and thanks to a spiral staircase that was three feet too wide for an octagonal soundstage, I had to fire the art director, rebuild the sets, and beg the record company for more money. In the very dark shadows of my runaway budget, I was encouraged to donate a fiscally responsible cameo performance, which many people have told me is "both sensuous and moving," if you don't count the fact that I'm wearing a size-sixteen polka-dot jumpsuit.

The concept for the video required that Madonna enact the role of a hot blonde actress who is pretending to covet superficiality, wealth, and power but who really yearns for depth, virtue, and big, hunky man-meat. Keith Carradine, who plays the Howard Hughes–type studio mogul, doesn't get with the program until the fourth chorus, third line, when he finally liquidates his assets in exchange for a stained wifebeater, a ripped leather jacket, and a dented pickup truck. True love, a hastily choreographed Portuguese tarantella, and the promise of petting below the waist rapidly ensue.

Actually, Mary Lambert had initially provided the record company with a *Lolita*-inspired concept in which Madonna carried a dolly, licked a lolly, and wriggled like a ferret on her stepdaddy's suspiciously bulging lap, but this idea was rejected as disgusting and immoral by the MTV censors, who found the idea of Madonna imitating an American sex kitten who choked on her own vomit after supposedly having sex with a married U.S. president and his brother much more in keeping with good old-fashioned rock video values.

Still, as you might have heard on David Letterman or *Behind the Music* or some other ancient deconstruct-the-celebrity television show, "Material Girl" was always meant to be *ironic*, because Madonna isn't *really* a material girl who *really* desires a famous actor, good-looking model, or successful movie director for a life partner—even though that may be what she always ends up with, because nobody ever gets it because nobody ever listens to the lyrics.

On the other hand, the tongue-in-cheek subtext may have been lost on her target audience, since at the time they were all seven-year-old girls. Yes, back in the weighty eighties a Madonna concert was packed to the rafters with thousands of hysterically overstimulated prepubescent females struggling not to wet their purple paisley hot pants as they hopped, skipped, and collectively mouthed the lyrics to "Like a Virgin" with their officially copyrighted rhinestone-encrusted Madonna crucifixes smacking against their tiny concave chests.

Of course, since the average elementary school student was still actually a virgin, because she had not yet been "touched for the very first time," there was something vaguely sinister about these product-laden "lootenannies"—the promise, perhaps, of the terrible Christmas Yet to Come when my own nine-year-old cherub would beg for a pair of Like a Genie Vinyl Thong Underpants just because she saw Christina Aguilera play an entire two-hour show with what looked like a pleather string inserted between her buttocks.

Back in the day, however, a girl was never too young for an old-time vaudeville role, and in a casting tour de force I landed the plum part of Boy Clown with Red Yarn on Head, while Madonna's best friend, Martin, played opposite me as the minxish Girl Clown with Mop-Top on Skull. Of course, we were widely admired for our courageous gender-ambivalent casting, but in truth Martin got the girl part because he fit into the size-two petite clown kilt and I didn't. Like everything else in life, one's rock video destiny is mathematically proportional to one's daily carbohydrate intake.

Actually, Martin proved surprisingly aggressive as a girl clown, and in a frenzy of comic improvisation he stuck his tongue in my mouth and wiggled it around. I did not feel this was professional behavior for a thespian, let alone for a "thelesbian," a noun that more adequately characterizes a young man wearing big red panties and a 44D cup. Still, our performances were inventive and hilarious, as I'm sure you'll agree if you look directly to the left, just outside the driver-side window of the brown pickup truck, during the scene on the studio backlot in which Madonna is making out with Keith Carradine.

That's me, two clowns to the right.

Earlier that day, Mo Austin, the legendary president of Warner Bros. Records, and Jeff Ayeroff, vice president of those in charge of my destiny, had come by the set to pay their respects. Of course, I made every attempt to sidle by without exciting attention, but it's hard to be discreet when you're wearing a red rubber nose.

"Hey everybody, look!" called Jeff to his exalted peer group. "That's Sharon Oreck, the line producer!"

Pivoting skillfully on my vast crimson clodhoppers, I paused to greet my elders with dignity. After all, clowns are not just losers who get knocked over by miniature poodles, plaid-bedecked midgets, and circus sluts in little red cars. They're a respected show business tradition representing a venerable performing art form that brings joy and laughter every year to millions of people with minimal IQs. Personally, I try never to be repulsed or frightened of clowns, unless, of course, they are also pedophiles or serial killers or people offering personality tests on Hollywood Boulevard.

"How do you do, Mr. Austin," I greeted him soberly. "I'm so very pleased to meet you."

Tipping my miniature green bowler cap, I tried to comport myself with the gravitas expected of a top-flight entertainment professional. On the other hand, Mr. Austin was the chief executive of a multinational corporation that catered to the intellectual, philosophical, and wardrobe standards of maladjusted adolescents. Maybe he wouldn't have a problem with forty-two-inch booties.

"Hah, Mo, whaddaya think?" Jeff broke in. "After the video, we can rent her out to birthday parties. It'll be part of the new Warner's austerity program."

Mo just nodded. To be fair, it was hard for anyone to focus when Madonna was frugging on set in a lustrous body-hugging pink *peau de soie* ensemble that defied any known technology for keeping her bosom in tow. Because despite the intervention of three kinds of glue, two brands of rubber cement, and one brief visit to the studio metal welder, the two-thousand-dollar steel-reinforced halter dress that had been meticulously copied and reconstructed from the nightclub scene in *Gentlemen Prefer Blondes* continued to waft gently into her lap every time Madonna hit the wiggle-wiggle-shimmy-pop at the end of the second-to-last chorus.

As the costume designer openly wept, production assistants were sent to scour the city for industrial adhesives, leaving the remaining crew to take an increasingly unwholesome interest in the fourth stanza's three-point backbend, when Madonna's twin orbs of flesh would inevitably begin to spasm, fidget, and finally gush forth from her hot pink bustier like freshly toasted Pop-Tarts vaulting into the persimmon hues of dawn.

With things busting out all over, it was bound to be spring and love was also in the air, thanks to a thoughtful production assistant who had offered to set Madonna up on a star-studded blind date with Sean Penn. Before you could say Entertainment Channel Special Announcement, the set was ablaze with rumors that this perfect couple would fall in love, get married, and have ten celebrity children just as soon as they actually met. Even the grips, who traditionally whiled away their free time comparing the density of their phlegm balls, were oohing and kvelling like little girls at a unicorn convention.

"He likes her! I can so tell by his expression!"

"Oh my God! They are perfect for each other!"

I hadn't seen this kind of collective immaturity since the fall of 1967, when Bobby Height had asked me to go steady in front of the Margate Junior High School Carom Pavilion. Even though he was three feet high, Robin Bacon insisted that I say yes, because Bobby was the cutest available guy in fourth-period lunch, and I was the cutest available girl in fifth. It would be a marriage of great dynasties, they explained, and the lunch periods would at last be united.

The Sean–Madonna union represented *exactly* the same kind of public demand on a personal relationship, minus the test afterward on the Constitutional Congress. With a creepy degree of insight, all anybody talked about all day long was how Sean and Madonna were going to get married, have fights, break up, make up, and then get divorced. According to the will of the people, the script about the Cool In-Crowd Rebel Actor and the Cool In-Crowd Rebel Pop Star had already been written, budgeted, and preapproved. Now it was up to the principal players to fuck like tigers, fight like pit bulls, and get on with our show.

• • •

One week into "Material Girl" production, I had come to the tragic conclusion that I could never be truly close to Madonna, mostly because I had never met her. That is because every time I made the least effort to enter her presence, Simon Fields would shove my clowny white ass right out the door. Maybe he felt I was not yet ready, or was way too ready, or was looking too much like Clarabelle the Cowgirl, or just maybe Simon was bogarting my superstar so he could keep her all to himself.

The truth was that before Sean, Madonna had been madly in love with Simon, and had even penned a song about his fabulous sense of humor and maverick fashion sense. Well, that's what I overheard the PA tell the sound guy that somebody said Simon had told the prop assistant. On the other hand, several members of the recently fired art department claimed to have spotted Prince's large purple converted school bus parked in front of Madonna's Hollywood Hills mansion, sparking rumors of a binding sexual alliance between two people who had no last names. Dear God, if they were actually to marry, how would we engrave the silver?

Of course, in the years to come, the legions of men, women, and others falsely claiming to have had at least one defining sexual experience with Madonna would be able to form their own peacekeeping alliance. To that end, I once had the strange good fortune to be riding in a van with six unbelievably handsome male Guess models who collectively appeared to be stupider than a single wooden hammer.

"What stuff you done?" challenged the first Adonis to the man-meat sitting next to him, ostensibly regarding work.

"Uh, you know, Calvin, uh, Madonna."

"You mean, like, a video?"

"Yeah. Yeah. Well, that too. Heh, heh, heh," he chortled insinuatingly.

"What? You did him? You did her?"

"Fuck you, dude! I'm not queer. I did her!"

"No way, dude! Me too."

Three minutes into our ride, five out of six models had an eleven-inch penis that had never been involved in an overtly homosexual experience, and seven minutes in they had all made sweet, sweet love to Madonna and had been begged for way more, doggie-style.

At this juncture, I feel I should go on record as an individual who has never made sweet, sweet love to Madonna. Furthermore, I have never heard her beg for more, doggie-style. On the other hand, I am a little deaf in my left ear, so maybe she did and I missed it.

It was on the last day of production that Simon finally took it upon himself to introduce me to the star of our show, who, with her lovely pink gown sliding down around her attractive pink torso, was in no position to criticize my adorable bobble hat. Likewise, she was in no mood to exchange phone numbers, talk about politics, or ask me where I got my forty-four-inch orange Afro wig. In point of fact, Madonna did not notice, pay attention to, or acknowledge me in any way whatsoever, probably because she already had enough friends, lovers, star-fuckers, hangers-on, personal assistants, and psycho stalkers to keep her busy for the three and a half minutes she had off every summer. On the other hand, she could have been one of the 76 percent of Americans who suspect clowns of being unhinged child rapists.

Meanwhile, even though I personally delivered a bag of macrobiotic lunch entrées and a Mars Bar to her personal Winnebago, Madonna continued not to notice me for three more videos, until a preproduction meeting for "Like a Prayer," when I accidentally caught her attention at a meeting by dropping a reference to my former career as a high school jezebel.

"*You* got pregnant at sixteen?" Madonna marveled, her voice trembling with awe and respect. Because although Madonna tried to act all cool, back when she had been a frilly, chilly, pom-pom queen, stretching her quads for the next big game at Michigan Freeze-Your-Ass-Off High, I had been balling my buns off in the empty weed lot next to Marineland under the merciless California sun.

Now we're making "Like a Prayer" and she's the one who's half-naked and crawling around the moss-covered cliffs of the South Bay.

"Wake up one of those fucking useless PAs and send them out to scour the community for a conscious medical professional who can bind Madonna's suppurating cacti wounds!" I bark at Hildy Inigborgasson, my executive producer, who gazes back at me with little hatchets of pure hate. "Also, find a 7-Eleven that's open and bring back six hundred gallons of black coffee! And send someone at once to go get the burning cross investigating team police officers some freshly baked glazed doughnuts! Er, also . . ." I add more quietly, "find a criminal production attorney who's up at 4:00 a.m. and give those cops a copy of our San Pedro location agreement with the official burning cross approval documents, assuming we actually have one. Oh, and dig up two free Madonna T-shirts and an album and give them to whoever the boss cop is."

There's a lot to do, but for now it's the only thing that'll keep us all awake, thanks to the junkie craft service chick who went missing at 1:00 a.m. with all the coffee. Fuming, I commit today's life lesson to memory: never allow a crazy crack bag who only gets paid $50 a day to leave the set with a hundred-dollar coffee pot. As the O in O Pictures, it's my duty to provide wisdom, stability, and leadership to a large group of psychologically unstable day laborers, so I'm supposed to know shit like that.

Meanwhile, I glower, seeing that Augustina, Mary Lambert's crazy assistant, has mowed down the rest of our bootlickers to arrive at Madonna's tattered feet with soothing unguents, warm towels, and an emergency medical kit miraculously in tow. When it comes to celebrities, Augustina seems to have magical control over space and time, so no matter who I assign to get Madonna a box of organic spelt flakes, a nonfat soy beverage, or a *National Enquirer* with Barbra Streisand being kidnapped by transgendered aliens on the cover, it will inevitably be she who shows up with the stuff.

This is creepy, not to mention an irritant to other, less-assertive star-fuckers, who get antsy, homicidal, and prone to charging me overtime whenever they are prevented from adequate one-on-one time with super-important pop divas. In a bold attempt to control employee overages, I have recommended that Augustina take a "celebrity interaction break," which requires a cessation of all physical (or psychic) contact with Madonna until the end of time, beginning right after she drives three hundred miles round-trip to find me some gum in, like, Palmdale.

Sadly, in our business, it isn't always possible to distinguish normal, run-of-the-mill show biz leeches from the bona fide, hyperdelusional celebrity stalkers, so it isn't until six months later that all the restraining orders have to be filed, after Augustina has informed everyone by registered mail that she is legally married to Liza Minnelli and will be performing an autobiographical two-woman show on Broadway with Phyllis Diller, or vice versa, depending on the day and—I'm just guessing here—the dosage.

Meanwhile, she is still here, introducing Madonna to a pair of twelve-inch medical tweezers by scissoring them menacingly in the air as she details her background as a professionally trained emergency technician with vast personal experience in cactus thorn–ectomy. Augustina, I've noticed, is extremely competitive regarding any form of injury or disease, and inevitably has had a worse case of whatever it is you have. She also claims to have training in every field of endeavor and has done every job, especially yours, at least once.

I consider objecting to her touching Madonna with a sharp instrument, then think, Aw, fuck it, let's throw her in the cage and see if she comes out alive. It's my opinion that a clumsy barb extraction performed at four in the morning on a world-acclaimed pop star could lead to a swift kick in the head, and I have to consider how much I might enjoy that. Nothing personal, but after nineteen hours of shooting I like to surrender to any fantasy that can accommodate my free-floating rage.

Besides, if we don't move soon, we'll have to schedule an extra day to shoot the "leap-of-faith" water sequence, which will require Madonna to plummet off a ten-meter diving platform and execute a slow-motion cannonball into an Olympic swimming pool that is twice as deep as the Atlantic Ocean and three times as expensive to rent by the hour. As Madonna's already impaled a major limb, lost all feeling in her outer extremities, and snapped one of her delicate fuck-me slip spaghetti straps, I make an executive decision that we might as well finish the day by drowning her at a new location.

"Okay, everybody! Let's move 'em out!" I shout as if I am personally ushering a great movement west. Dead or alive, these li'l dogies will finish as one. Of course, some of us may soon be deader than others. After all, we are about to push the world's number-one pop star off a three-story ledge without a rehearsal, and she hasn't slept in two days. Normally, this sort of thing would cheer me up, but I was really starting to like her. I mean, there's *no* question. She *will* die.

I hate this. It's stupid and I'm completely convinced that we'll never use it. I've been trying all week to get Mary to cancel it, but she continues to insist that it's a vital adjunct to the "plunging-into-grace" dream sequence, during which Madonna will attempt to convey the unique commingling of religious and sexual sensations that occurs when she falls in very slow motion through super-fluffy cumulus clouds.

This is *exactly* the kind of pseudoreligious biracial sex-positive save-the-world softcore porn fantasy that is engendered in pre-teen girls when burgeoning levels of estrogen are released into the central nervous system during a very long Latin mass. Just ask Mary and Madonna, two chicks personally named for the mother

of God—what good is a spiritual epiphany without a little burning, burning love?

Unfortunately we may never know, because the "Big Jump" is
running behind schedule, because we have had to cram the con-
joined plot points of the New Testament, the *Kama Sutra*, and
Mandingo into four and a half measly days of shooting, because
Warner Bros. doesn't want to pay three times what the entire U.S.
House of Representatives makes every four years for another
twelve hours of production.

By "days," I refer here to "video days," which have come to be
defined as any single time period beginning immediately after the
crew starts working until the exact time that they decide to kill
Mary and me. Now, after we've been shooting for seventy-two
hours straight, I have the unenviable task of prodding that very
same crew, not to mention Madonna, to wrap out this location
and convoy forty minutes to the U.S.C. training pool, where we
will have forty minutes to set up, shoot, and wrap before the U.S.
Olympic diving team shows up to throw us out on our soggy rock
video asses.

Against my better judgment, I go over to the superstar wagon
to lecture Madonna on why it's not necessarily fatal to be dropped
on your head into a large receptacle of L.A. tap water at four in
the morning. Finding Augustina just outside her door, I send
her out on a philanthropic mission to find soy cookies for Madonna. Then I enter to find Madonna pulling cactus thorns out of
her toes.

"So, um, Madonna, did you know that pearl divers in the Mal-
dives often leap from heights of up to eighty feet into shallow
ponds in order to display their prowess for prospective mates?" I
lie with Talmudic authority. "The percentage of spinal column in-
juries is surprisingly low."

"Right." Madonna cuts me off before I even get a chance to
grovel. "Let's go."

Tears instantly well up in my eyes, a sure sign that we are rounding the seventy-second working hour, when all my rage mystically transmutes to mush.

"Omigod, Madonna!" I sob. "No matter how much we torture you, you're always ready for more. You are indomitable. A goddess. A standard bearer. A rock."

Madonna's jaw twitches. She's bored shitless and would like to take a bath before the millennium is over.

"Okay already," she barks. "Let's do it. Now."

Woof.

Yessir.

Hitching a ride to the location in Madonna's two-mile-long, filthy, dirty luxury Star Wagon, I experience a mini anxiety attack while watching her burrow under a bouncing pile of blankets, quilts, sweaters, jackets, and socks. She appears to be blue, and I don't mean depressed blue, I mean freezing-cold-hypothermia blue. As I have already chewed off most of my lower lip, I seek comfort in a couple of glazed doughnut holes that I find in my coat pocket. Then, nibbling on an organic butter pat that I find at the back of Madonna's mini fridge, I move to the front seat and light up back-to-back Marlboros. Hey, who needs an aorta? I'm about to kill the patron saint of little girls who wear bullet bras. By tomorrow I'll be dead, shot down in the prime of life by vengeful preadolescent mini ninjas.

Defying my gothic mindscape, we arrive at the pool location to find that the sun is up and the sky is blue. A suddenly pert Mary goes with the cameraman to set up the shot. Madonna comes out of her trailer, looking refreshed. I look up at the diving platform.

Well. Whaddaya know. It doesn't look *that* far away.

My heart soars.

"So *that's* ten meters?" I say gleefully.

Everyone looks up. Everyone agrees. Madonna will live after all!

"Thank you, Jesus, Mary, and Joseph . . ." I intone softly, even though I was a big Jew earlier that day.

We are ready.

Madonna climbs up the ladder with the Olympic diving team coach, whom we have employed at a very great price to provide very great technical advice.

"*Prepare the shot!*" yells the assistant director.

"*Roll the playback!*" yells the assistant's assistant.

"*Let's do it!*" encourages the director.

"*Turn on the jets!*" orders the diving coach.

Somebody presses a big red button on a big white pole, which suddenly prompts giant waves to undulate through the pool, making a scary sucking sound. Our pristine Olympic natatorium has been instantly transformed into the world's loudest and weirdest Jacuzzi.

"*Cut, cut, cut!*" screams the assistant director.

"*What the fuck?*" screams the director.

Bewildered, I whip out my walkie-talkie and, after the usual ten attempts, figure out which button to push.

"Uh . . . what's going on? Why is the, uh, water screaming?"

"Uh, this is what we do with beginners," explains the coach. "It softens the water. Over."

I am confused. Why do we have to "soften" the water? Isn't it already a liquid?

Meanwhile, out at the end of the diving platform, we can see the diving coach gesticulating wildly, making a falling-leaf motion with his right hand that emits an audible *splat!* when it meets his left one.

He appears to be demonstrating the *wrong* way to jump off a diving platform.

After ten failed attempts to raise the coach on my radio, I throw the fucking thing in the pool and climb the three-story diving ladder myself. I don't really think about what I'm doing until I'm there and a strange thing happens: the saliva dries up in my mouth, my eyes roll back in my head, and I fall like a bag of bananas to the board.

Whatever I do, I must not stand up. More important, I must not fall down. I look around. The landscape is pulsing like the artery in my neck. Don't look around. I look down. The water is boiling like the terror in my heart. Don't look down.

I look up. Madonna is staring at me like I'm a big fat baby clutching a diving board.

"Are you . . . uh, okay?" she asks.

"Er, oh yeah, sure," I lie vigorously, nails bleeding as they claw the diving board. I'm a leader, a titan of industry. I must not be seen as a feeble, gutless pantywaist, vomiting panic from on high.

"I'm simply, er, checking the structural integrity of this surface."

"Right," Madonna quips with thinly veiled disgust. "Can you please get out of the way now?"

"Well . . . not really."

It's not that I wouldn't be glad to help out, but my arms and legs are no longer taking orders from my brain. Turns out, I'm scared of heights.

Shaking her head, Madonna coolly steps around me and climbs down the ladder. I consider waving, but then I reject the notion as I realize it would require me to unwrap my fingers from the board.

Ten or fifteen minutes later, after a friendly sound man pries my hands loose from the platform I figure out how to get to ground level intact and find the crew and cast in the middle of a serious discussion as to whether Madonna will die if she jumps off the plat-form or just break her head open like a ripe casaba melon. I ask the diving coach for his professional opinion and expertise.

"I believe that Madonna *will not die*," he solemnly announces, "as long as she jumps *out* toward the water—that is—not *in*, toward the concrete."

I am not reassured.

"Why don't you show us how *not* to jump *in* toward the concrete?" I snidely suggest.

He looks uncomfortable. "I didn't bring my trunks."

I turn around and find Augustina, somehow back from the soy Oreo run. She's excited, her eyes are dilated, and she's wriggling like a badger in a potato sack.

"I'll jump off the platform! I'll show her how! I'll show her that it's safe!" Augustina gurgles, her throat catching on the thrill of risking her whole life for one quarter-millisecond of Madonna's halfhearted attention. "Really! It's so easy! I've done it thousands of times."

I look at Mary. She looks at me.

I look at Madonna. She looks at me.

I look at Augustina.

"Really! I want to do it! I was number one on the Yale diving team!" Augustina continues.

"Perhaps you have forgotten that you are not wearing your swimsuit, dear," I suggest through clenched teeth.

"I don't need a bathing suit! I'll do it in my clothes!"

Before I get the opportunity to say, *Augustina, are you fucking nuts?* she is climbing up the pool ladder, proving it once again.

Even though I am profoundly concerned for the health and safety of all my crew members, I can't help but reflect that Augustina's feigned swimming capabilities have conspired to make her the perfect lab rat. If, for instance, she should manage to land in the pool incorrectly (as in *away* from the water and *toward* certain death), Madonna will have to assume that even an Ivy League collegiate champion is incapable of making such a dive safely, which will lead her to demand a special-effects alternative, preferably a cheap one, like dropping Malibu Barbie into a bucket.

On the other hand, it's just not right to allow Augustina to commit suicide, even if she is a clinically insane celebrity stalker who is being paid to not do what she's told. She is still a person, entitled to freedom, liberty, and a full lifespan. Besides, if I let all the crew members who are annoying, disrespectful, and clinically insane kill themselves for Madonna, there will be nobody left to wrap out the equipment.

"Ready or not, here I come!" shouts Augustina, tearing down the gangplank.

"Come down from there this instant!" I yell sternly. "Or mark my words! You will be in very big trouble, young lady!"

Augustina totally ignores me, gives a big thumbs-up to Madonna, and jumps off to take the plunge.

Then, as if in a Wile E. Coyote cartoon sketched by Francis Bacon, we see Augustina's gray trench coat plummet three stories, her legs skittering and twitching as she throttles through space with a stifled scream distorting her features, until she crashes into the water flat on her back, with a sickening *kersplatt!*

Oops.

The diving coach looks grim. This is apparently *not* the way to jump off a ten-meter diving platform.

For a long moment, we search the water for signs of life.

Then Augustina surfaces, spitting, paddling, and panting. Omigod, she is alive! She drags herself slowly out of the pool as I bring her a towel and lightly pat her back, now the color of a ripe summer plum.

"Fllfahl grht," Augustina exclaims as her eyes roll around in her head like lotto balls. "Grghkk?"

As she is carried off to the medical Winnebago, the diving coach explains to Madonna that Augustina has just demonstrated the exact technique for sustaining a permanent spinal injury and irreversible neurological damage.

Hmmmm. Madonna listens carefully. Then she decides she is going to do the shot anyway. After all, there is no way some Yalie stalker chick is gonna one-up the Queen of Pop!

Madonna mounts the platform after goodbye hugs to the makeup and hair team who, I swear to God, are crying.

Mary uses the bullhorn to issue last-minute instructions. "Okay, Madonna, this is the dream sequence!"

Madonna takes her position at the end of the diving board. She shivers in her fuck-me slip. Her hands are wadded into tight little balls.

"Remember: you are blissful, ecstatic, and serene!"

Madonna nods stiffly. Tears roll down her exhausted cheeks.

"Roll camera!" calls Mary.

Because we are shooting at six hundred frames per second, the camera has to be in motion for thirty seconds before it can get up to running speed, after which film starts burning like Malibu in August.

"A-a-and . . . action!" Mary shouts.

Madonna perches at the edge of the platform for some time. Then, there's a splash. Then, we can't see her. Then, she is at the side of the pool, climbing out.

The water pressure has done its job. The top of her slip has dropped to her waist, and the bottom of the slip has risen to her hips, so Madonna is now totally wet and totally naked, if you don't count the bulging sash of sopping brown silk bunched up around her abdomen.

The crew cheers and slaps one another five. She is Venus rising, sans the half shell.

I'm not saying whether she is a natural blonde.

"Nice work, Madonna! You're the best! It looked practically a lot like you weren't even a total amateur!" I scream enthusiastically as she exits the pool, hyperventilating, and tries to fold herself into a fetal position.

"So whaddaya think?" I continue, oblivious to the signs of her stress. "Do you feel like you got the shot or do you want to try aga—?"

"No, no, no! There will not be a fucking second take!"

The crew cheers again. More high fives.

Madonna jumps into her powder-blue Mercedes and speeds off into the Los Angeles smog. Augustina is taken to the hospital. I jump in the pool in all my clothes to show everyone what a good sport I am.

I get the flu.

Two days later I recline in a sleek ergonomic lounge chair in the dark recesses of telecine bay three at Unitel Video, where we've come to transfer the "Like a Prayer" dailies from motion picture film to videotape. In the old days—before the video playback system enabled the entire crew to see exactly what the camera was seeing—this was the first time you got to see what you had actually shot.

The air is heavy with anticipation. After color-correcting and video-manipulating three days worth of footage ("Can you double up the flames on crucifix four?" "Can you give the whole image a pervasive sense of impending doom?"), we finally come to the "Madonna's leap-of-faith" sequence, in which we shoved her off the diving platform just before dawn so she could portray a moment of sexual-spiritual surrender while floating gently through brilliant morning skies.

Mary and I fill up our popcorn boxes and take the phones off the hook. This is when our real life finally turns into a movie.

INT. – TELECINE BAY 3 – ENDLESS NIGHT

Madonna is perched on a diving platform thirty feet above the water. Her eyes are closed. Her fists are clenched. Tears stream down her face.

MARY (screaming off-screen)
We're rolling! *Jump!*

Madonna's mummified, as if she's rehearsing for rigor mortis. Despite Mary's entreaties, she remains glued to the platform. She waits. She prays. She weeps.

MARY (*really* screaming off-screen)
Jump! Now!

Madonna's eyes are tightly closed as she faces inward, observing the ancient battle between the tiny brain angel who says it's way fucking stupid to jump off a three-story ledge and the tiny mind demon who says she's man enough to do it.

MARY (*really psycho*, screaming off-screen)
Madonna! The fucking camera is running! Jump and we'll let you go home!

This promise finally jolts Madonna into action, and she carefully crosses herself before stepping off the platform into the rosy hues of dawn. Naturally, this is *also* exactly the same exact moment when camera one runs out of film.

There is a deep, penetrating silence in telecine bay three.

I look at Mary. She's not laughing. Very bad sign. I offer an exploratory snigger. She doesn't join in. I pretend it was a cough.

Well, there's always the footage from camera two. Maybe I should be praying to my own god. Lacking references, I vigorously hum "Hava Nagila" to myself. Sure enough, the operator from camera two is a wily fellow who disobeyed orders and held his roll until something actually happened. So, close up and in extreme slow motion, he's been able to capture Madonna as she soars majestically through space.

Hallelujah. I mean, *Baruch Atah Adonai.*

But wait, halt, and hold yer ding-dang rabbinical socks.

Because what we see is *not* America's number-one sex symbol soaring with tingling religiosity through the fluffy dawn skies of her interior paradise. Because what we see is *not* the coolest girl in contemporary pop culture embracing the dangers of life, love, and liberty with the heart, spirit, and bubble butt of a feminist warrior in a fuck-me slip. Because what we see is *not* the living metaphor for modern existence, multiple orgasms, and maniacal self-interest risking it all by soaring through space for truth, justice, and the American way.

Nope, through the miracle of modern slow-motion single-frame film technology, what we see instead is a scared-as-shit, totally exhausted, wet-rat, contemporary pop diva who would really like to go home to her multimillion-dollar Bel Air mini-mansion, so she can count her gold bullion, paint Homer Winslow seascapes, fuck Warren Beatty, eat tofu cupcakes, and quit all this rock video bullshit forever. In the meantime, she is silently but unmistakably screaming foul and nonbroadcastable profanities with her mouth wide open and her dress flying off as she drops like a lead balloon past three dozen fat, ugly construction workers, two farting grips, and the damp, concerned faces of the makeup and hair people, and then disappears like a melted snow cone beneath the roiling water of what is quite clearly signposted as the U.S.C. athletic department swimming pool.

MADONNA (falling)
SHIIIIITFUUUUUCKHEEEEELL! (*Kersplash!*)

I look at Mary. She's still not laughing. Really, really bad sign.
"Reshoot?" I whimper.
Mary looks at me. She thinks.
"Nah," she finally replies. "We don't really need it."

13

In the Meantime

kay, so I was out on my own. Cast out. Forsaken. Kicked out of my house, deserted by friends, estranged from family—finally I had a destiny to pursue. According to chapter six of my Florence Crittenton *Great Moments in Western Civilization* eleventh-grade workbook, brilliant artists, burgeoning writers, and bright-eyed visionaries were always forsaken by their parents, steeped in poverty, and shunned by society.

Meanwhile, as long as I was willing to attend high school or college, I would be allowed to leech off the taxpaying public by receiving $232 a month, plus food stamps and minimal medical care. In that vein, I would henceforth be required to show up once a month at a piss-stinking, filth-encrusted West Los Angeles welfare office to expound on why I was such a useless, slatternly parasite who was wasting the capital resources of the great state of California. Every time I did this, I had to consider the possibility that welfare might be worse than getting a job.

My baby boy was six weeks old by the time I got a cheap apartment to bring him home to. Nobody wanted me to keep him, so nobody helped me to do so. I had waged unilateral thermonuclear war against my parents, the state welfare system, and all common sense. My reward was twenty-one inches long.

I named him Joshua David, and for the first thirty-six hours after I brought him home, I was the happiest teen trollop in America. Then I settled down to become the exhausted, bedraggled hag I would remain for the next ten years.

Because guess what? My new infant child just did not seem impressed that I had recently pushed his great big head out of my little tiny vagina and was now really in the mood for big naps, long pedicures, and delicious buns and cakes being served to me in bed. Instead, *he* was demanding to be bounced and bottled and snuggled and strollered and *googoo*ed and *gaagaa*ed every single hour of every single day. Obviously, Josh was too young to understand how his unrelenting personal needs put a serious crimp on my sleeping all day and going to pot parties all night. In this way, he was exactly like my parents, although less experienced with solids.

Whatever. He was way cute and his head smelled like God. Besides, if I tried to return him, my mom and dad would just force me back to Miraleste High School, where Miss Magnetron, my closet lesbian guidance counselor, was eagerly waiting to display me at freshmen tutorials on the dangers of intercourse.

The only problem was that my life was a hellhole and every day I waited for the next crisis to occur. Toilet backed up. Diaper rash. Eviction notice. Oven explosion. Dented fenders. Job firing. Colic. Pinkeye. Bad dates. Cockroaches. Stalkers. Subpoenas. Head lice. Gas turned off. Water turned off. Light turned off. Phone turned off. Thrown rod. Butt worms. Broken teeth. Double pneumonia. You name the pain, we had it, wholesale.

No problem. Even as I was buried alive, I breathed deep. I understood the turmoil to be the prequel to my *real* life. At any moment, the chaos of my hand-to-mouth existence, the sense of impending doom, the gnawing at the pit of my stomach, would be replaced by my correct fate, the one with grace and a washing machine.

Until then, my only option was to wade deeper into the muck.

Adhering to my strict bad-relationship policies, I continued to date any insensitive person with a scrotum within a hundred square miles. As a consequence, no man I went out with through the late seventies was fit for intimacy, employment, or carrying on a conversation about anything besides his own semen. At this juncture I would like to add that I did not have a real orgasm until I was twenty-two years old. This is pathetic only if you consider the twenty thousand guys I had sex with before that.

Meanwhile, maintaining a small child, a sporadic employment history, and a pitiable love life kept me so busy that before I knew it I was twenty. I had made it past my teens, but the entirety of my assets now consisted of one four-year-old boy, two used Oriental carpets, and my dad's donated fecal-brown Ford LTD that looked exactly like a seventies narc car, at least to the smack dealers who kept throwing eggs at it when his office was down on Western and Adams.

In search of a better way of life, I decided to take the narc car and move up the freeway so I could sign up for free film classes at Los Angeles City College, the proletarian answer to higher education. Hey, maybe in the heart of the city I would meet people who did something besides take acid and go to the beach. Maybe I could learn something that wasn't stupid, boring, or reliant on illegal pharmaceutical products to make it modestly entertaining. Maybe I would discover my raison d'être, or at least how to spell it.

Film school turned out to be just the ticket, except for the part where it took twelve of the twenty-four hours I needed every day to keep my four-year-old child from leaping off balconies, catching baseballs with his teeth, and testing electrical sockets with his index fingers. Because my brilliant little baby got up every morning at dawn to be the healthiest, hardiest, most super-active human male child in the whole entire world.

"*Och*, he's all boy, the little dickens," emoted his Irish pediatrician, Dr. Honoria Hardy. "He'll keep ya busy day and night, dontcha know!"

I didn't see her staying home to look after her own nine little leprechauns, *och* aye and begorra.

Still, Josh was a stunning, towheaded moppet, with the eyes of a Keene painting and a very big brain. A verbal wunderkind, he never shut his mouth from the moment he figured out how to open it, and the two of us began a lifetime of interrupting each other that continues to this day. He was such a charming baby that even my parents forgot that he was a personal problem and fell madly in love with him, as did the parents of his conceptual artist father, who sadly continued to be a Weasel until very recently, when he finally emerged from decades of amnesia to recall that he had gotten drunk and utterly abandoned his infant child thirty-six years earlier. Oops.

Life continued apace until one hot summer's day in 1977, right after I had picked a number to wait for five and a half hours in a melting plastic chair with a suspicious brown stain on the seat, when I had a life-altering epiphany.

"Welfare sucks!" I screamed thoughtfully, while watching a filthy two-year-old child piss through her dissolving paper diaper right onto my left foot. "It's over!"

"Number four hundred and fifty-two!" sputtered the loudspeaker as I stormed out the door and jumped into my car.

The truth was that it *was* over. It was no longer *mandatory* for me to live like a cheap welfare slut just because I was one. I mean, c'mon, it was practically the eighties! It was no longer fashionable to be impoverished, depressed, and pathetic. Young people were no longer expected to look like shit and live like shit and drive ugly cars and have poxy boyfriends who treated them like a rash on a scab on the butt of a poodle.

I would change my life. I would get a real over-the-counter job that paid real over-the-counter government-taxed money. I would be rich. I would be powerful. And nobody would ever urinate on my foot again!

Throwing the car into first gear, I resolved to get off the poverty track right there and right then. Then I noticed in my rearview mirror that a battered green Toyota sedan was tailing me very, very closely.

"Fucking welfare people!" I fumed, having been off the public rolls for almost twenty seconds already. Then I looked in my mirror a little more closely and noticed that there was no driver. Now that was odd.

I was just starting to believe that acid flashbacks weren't a great big lie manufactured by alien robots who were secretly employed by the Nixon administration when a screaming family of Ukrainian immigrants brought it to my attention that I was driving off with their much-used Toyota Celica attached to my rear bumper.

Whoops.

Bad parallel parking technique.

Pulling over with loud apologies in what I hoped to be some intelligible form of Slavic, I joined the Kalinowski clan in jumping on my bumper to set their vehicle free, taking the opportunity to symbolically detach myself from the California welfare system. Then, as I waved goodbye to Chad, Vlad, and their ten little Dimitris, I waved goodbye to state assistance. It had been great, but now it was time to hit the big time, or at least the little time, or at least something that wasn't nothing time.

From then on, I took any job that was not at the phone company: I typed letters, I delivered papers, I spun blood plasma on a centrifuge, folded dungarees at a children's clothing shop, answered phones. I filed. I clerked. I cleaned. I cooked.

The temptation to stop motivated me forward—I knew that if I lay down I would never get up again. I fell asleep at the wheel on my way to my 5:00 a.m. job. I totaled my car and got arrested for not paying my traffic tickets. I waited to pay my utilities until the day they were shut off. I "borrowed" T-bones from the Lucky Market. I got my clothes from garage sales. I lifted towels from the public pool. I was perpetually exhausted, sick, and poor, but for me there was no question.

I would triumph at something, somehow, someday. In the meantime, I kept getting fired.

My bosses hated me. I was aggressive. I was belligerent. I couldn't take orders. I wouldn't do what I was told. I didn't show up on time. I swiped the inventory. I broke the register. I stuck blood samples in the urine drawer. I filed the *R*s in the *T*s. I drafted new policies.

In other words, I demonstrated what would be known in the eighties as *leadership skills*! In short, I exemplified exactly the kind of supercharged, self-possessed, aggressive employee profile that I would scrupulously avoid and repudiate the minute I had the chance to hire people myself.

As a born outsider with no real training, background, or education, there was only one business for me: show business.

In July 1977, through a friend of a friend who was so important that he knew a grip who worked in Hollywood, I obtained a twenty-five-dollar-*a-week* position as a fake grip/electrician on *Cindy Lou and the Texas Turnaround*, the first and last Chuck Norris picture to explore the inherent existential tension between Zen Buddhism and hammering the shit out of crazy incestuous truck pirates.

The one-sheet movie poster, which you can bring up right now on the Internet Movie Database, tells the whole story with a bold black-lettered tagline that reads "One Man Can Make a Difference!" right under a brightly colored picture of Chuck Norris kicking a uniformed police officer in the throat.

From this, you might deduce that a top creative force on this movie had strong negative "vibes" toward what used to be known in the seventies as "the pigs." On the other hand, you might suspect that a crackhead without portfolio might have been imbibing a twice-daily ration of animal tranquilizers and should not have been left in charge of marketing and publicity.

In any case, the movie was eventually reborn as *Breaker! Breaker!* right after American International Pictures decided that the first title had too many letters in it to put on the marquee.

Note: The film was later released in Poland as *Zabijaka! Zabijaka!*

Although my grip duties on *Breaker!* fell mostly in the areas of hauling, schlepping, and procuring cold beverages for disgusting, lecherous karate dudes, I was also paid twenty-five dollars a week to hold the microphone, drop the film off at the lab, and play the part of Flo, the heartbroken widow of Texas Town's beloved garbageman.

"You kilt my Wade!" I was ordered to scream at Mr. Norris while throttling him violently about the chest.

"Louder, honey!" our director yelled at me, in between whiffs from a small steel canister. "And hit him with hard-er-ness!"

Our leader suffered from the worst case of unmerited, multi-faceted self-confidence that I have ever seen. On the other hand, he had four houses, two girlfriends, and three wives. I realized then that it didn't matter if you were good at your job, as long as you had the right job. Because everybody kissed the director's big nitric booty, except, of course, my dear friend and co–fake grip/electrician, Margaret Goldsmith, who had been raised by her left-leaning parents to fight injustice, share the wealth, and stick it to the man before he stuck it to her first.

"I'm not your fucking baby!" Marge snorted huffily when the director ordered her to move a C-stand with his typical oppressive, male chauvinist–type endearments. "And keep your eyes off my breasts!"

Margaret was a pistol. Of course, that's why I got to play Flo and she had to go pick up the ice. Sadly, although I performed my role loudly and with great hard-er-ness, my part got cut because the camera ran out of film and somebody had forgotten to buy more.

14

In the (Stupid) Closet

Hey, you! Hold your bitch ass up there!"

Following a long, frustrated attempt to obtain unwholesome snack products at the Sikh vegetarian good-karma craft service table, I'm skulking back to the "In the Closet" video production vehicle, clutching an unsweetened nonfat tempeh cookie, when I happen to notice that I'm being verbally assaulted by two enormous thugs who are senior members of the Michael Jackson "In the Closet" security team.

"Where do you think yer goin'?" barks Enormous Thug #1.

"Yeah . . ." agrees Enormous Thug #2. "Don't be stupid. You need to stop *now* or face the immediate *consguences!*"

"Ummmm, guys, it's *meeeee*," I say, hopefully. "Remember? The *producer*?"

I try to place a sober emphasis on my respected company owner status by tightening my sphincter muscles and emanating a proud supreme commander–type aura, whereupon Thug #1 pushes back his sunglasses so I can better watch him roll his eyes.

"Never saw you before, don't see ya now."

"Nope, me neither," agrees Thug #2. "Now fuck off and go away."

Thug #1 waves his hand, formally dismissing me until the end of all time. Thug #2 concurs.

Neither bothers to unroot himself from either one of their low-slung purple plaid plastic beach chairs, from which they stand, or rather *sit* guard over a bizarre, makeshift alleyway of twisted black curtain material that is stretched across an entire quarter mile of the Palm Desert salt flats.

Because this surreal construct, which was erected five days ago from C-stands, grip clips, and twenty-by-thirty-foot swatches of night-black Duvateen, provides the draped corridor of night that will allow Michael Jackson to pass in complete personal privacy from his trailer to the "In the Closet" video set, where two hundred and fifty hot, bored crew members are waiting to cover their eyes and twiddle their thumbs because M.J. demands that no eyes can be upon him while he thrusts his scrawny, internationally renowned pelvis in the general direction of supermodel Naomi Campbell, who is dancing around a brown Tibetan yak named Gurkum while three grown men frantically shadow her with handheld 16 mm Arriflex cameras.

"I advise you not to keep standing around here," Thug #1 snipes at me, mostly because I just keep standing around there, because I'm trying to figure out how to sneak behind them so I can get back to my production vehicle.

"Yeah, Mr. Jackson gave *spelifif* orders. No one can look at him unless necessary," Thug #2 warns, menacingly shaking what appears to be a delicious fat-engorged Kentucky Fried Chicken leg at me.

For a guy who regularly takes hold of his nutsac in order to wag it around in front of fifty thousand paying customers, Michael sure pays a lot of people a lot of money to make sure he avoids prying eyes. Then again, I have to consider that the Michael Jackson universe includes regular press releases declaring that his nose has grown miraculously slimmer while his skin has grown mysteriously whiter while his chin has spontaneously been riven by a deep, previously undetected cleft that is a natural part of the normal process of the typical puberty of a thirty-one-year-old man who regularly has sleepovers with eleven-year-old boys.

Then I vainly attempt to explain my position as executive producer to Thugs #1 and #2.

"You guys. I'm the *owner* of O Pictures! I'm the boss of the set, don't you remember? We've been here together all week!"

"The boss? *Hoo hoo hah hah!*"

The air is sprayed with a fine mist of chicken breading as the Thugs consider my ridiculous allegations. Because if I'm the boss, why don't I have my own security team? Where are my six entertainment attorneys, seven copyright lawyers, and criminal litigation team? What about my two management firms, my private biker-chick dermatological nurse, and my chimp wearing his standard French artist beret and diapers? Where are all my little friends with all of their little friends, who are all former television, pop music, and movie child stars? Where is my motorcade, my gun-wielding personal bodyguard, my plastic-surgery-identical photo double, and my core audience base of nineteen million screaming fans?

"No, really, guys," I insist to the Thugs, who are now falling out of their beach chairs from laughing so hard. "I need to be on the set. It's my job."

"Well, it's our job not to let nobody on this set," replies Thug #2. "So stop talking. Now."

Finally Thug #3 prances over to get some coleslaw and inadvertently comes to my rescue.

"Oh yeah, she okay. She works for that director guy. The queer."

"*You* work for the Irv Schlitz Company?" questions Thug #1.

"Oh yeah, I thought she looked familiar," confesses Thug #2, a hazy memory rising like the moon in his antediluvian cortex.

I jam my thumb between my teeth, trying to staunch the invective that is threatening to rise like a gas bubble out of my larynx. Because it's Ritts, not Schlitz, and it's Herb, not Irv, and he's not queer—well, he *is*, but don't call him that—and fourth, it's my company, not his, and fifth . . . did I mention that I'm *the boss*?

Apparently not. Oh well. I force a big, fat smile onto my face.

"Okay. Yes. I *do* work for, ahem, Mr. Schlitz. May I go on the set now?"

"Oh, okay, sorry, miz. Go ahead. Hey, Dom!" Thug #1 yells to Thug #4, who is eating pizza in another purple plaid beach chair, ten feet down the corridor. "Let her through. She's the Shitz's assistant!"

I pretend to be thankful while making a mental note to seek balance in the galaxy by humiliating someone very soon.

Meanwhile, I am surprised that I cannot immediately locate the two hundred and fifty crew members I left here, alive and sweating in the one-hundred-degree heat, about seventeen minutes ago. With mounting alarm, I retrace my steps past the now familiar on-set landmarks:

1. The *My Dinner with Michael* African elephant stable
2. The sixteenth-century Catholic mission church ruins with lotsa Christs-on-a-cross thingies
3. The Chinese peacock and California vulture aviary enclosure
4. The squalid Latino version of an Oktoberfest dance hall
5. The sleeping great beasts of prey lion pen
6. The Guatemalan gushing water fountain
7. The village meeting square with imported Peruvian dirt clumps and pebbles area
8. The South African single-humped camel and llama caravan
9. The hall of fake closets desert drydock
10. The rainforest village flamenco dancing girl practice barre

Then, as I come out from behind the Tibetan yak imported grass grazing area, I inadvertently stumble upon the giant water-wheel sex dance action zone, where several hundred grips, gaffers, camera operators, art assistants, and pseudo-Aztec dance extras are all doing *nothing* as they sit around on melting camera cases trying to keep the saliva from drying up in their mouths by sucking on the corners of their "In the Closet" plastic security badges.

"What in the name of all that is motherfucking holy is going on around here?" I demand of Scott, the fair-skinned assistant director, who has recently turned the color of a little red wagon. As if in direct answer to my prayers for balance, the great Creator has already sent me somebody to pick on. Praise Allah, there is a karma god!

Scott doesn't even bother to look up from his *Hollywood Reporter* as he points to the fake shady oak arbor next to the flaming jugglers practice area, where Herb Ritts is being interviewed by Cindy Crawford for *MTV News*.

"Oh."

From forty feet away I can see Herb's teeth glinting in the sun as he shoves his tanned, Miami-de-viced puss into the television cameras.

Omigod. The only thing Herb loves more than performing minimal services for maximum fees is free press. If I don't go over there and forcibly extract him, our staff will burn up and blow away, like the singed petals of a recently torched sunflower.

"Sorry, Scott," I mumble as I head over.

Scott doesn't even look up again as he raises his hand to flip me off. Clearly there is a wrinkle in the fabric of universal justice.

"Uh, Herb, can I talk to you for a second?" I interrupt.

Herb is in the middle of telling Cindy Crawford how *he* came up with the "In the Closet" concept, so he completely ignores me, not to mention the other fifteen people who got paid several thousands of dollars to spend several hundreds of hours pouring through every single visual, musical, fashion, and literary reference in the entire world in order to come up with one single idea for getting Michael Jackson to do something in this video besides grab his dick and moonwalk on the beach.

Deeply irritated, I start to chant Herb's fake name in an annoying Yiddish accent, ten or twenty times in a row.

"Irv Schlitz, Irv Schlitz, Irv Schlitz . . . ," etc.

Herb's glowing press smile immediately dissolves into a glowering scowl the second Cindy turns away to answer a phone call.

"Why are you calling me that?" he hisses.

"It's a joke, Herb," I whine.

"It's *not* funny."

He slams *not* hard.

"Sorry, Herb," I apologize, secretly elated. I've recently had reason to hate Herb, and he's not an easy man to get revenge upon. Unfortunately, we have more important things to do right now than get on each other's nerves.

"We've got to get back to work, Herb. Can't you do this interview later? Everyone's melting."

"No," Herb replies primly, "I cannot. This interview is very important, both to my work and to Michael Jackson's."

"LikeIgiveashit," I mumble, Janet Jackson style.

Herb and I have a glare-off, which I'm stupid enough to think I might've won, for the one second that it takes me to realize he's just thought of something unpleasant for me to do instead.

"Oh, I forgot to tell you . . ." he adds, his tone softening. "We have a 'problem.'"

Uh-oh. When Herb says "we" have a "problem," what he usually means is "you" have a "problem," which almost always means me.

"What kind of a 'problem'?" I ask suspiciously.

Lately, any mention of a "problem" has been immediately followed by a mandatory forty-five-minute lecture on why Herb deserves to earn more money than God and to have his boyfriend come to every location in order to hold his glasses case, which is why he needs a bigger hotel suite than me.

"Just go talk to Naomi."

Ewww-god. A *Naomi* "problem."

Naomi is full of the kind of "problems" that almost make me nostalgic to discuss Herb's corporate tax status, profit-share ratio, and raise-in-daily-salary "problems."

Let me explain.

The latest Naomi "problem" had occurred two and a half hours earlier, right after I was summoned by a panicked walkie-talkie call to the picnic bench outside her dressing room trailer, where a knockdown brawl had recently taken place between her and prominent members of the hair-and-makeup team.

"Dear God! What's happened here?" I asked as I arrived at her Star Wagon. I'd been around, but I'd never seen two grown men crying and beating their fists against the walls of a recreational vehicle before.

"Oh, Sharon, it was terrible!" trembled George, the sensitive, softspoken, porcelain-hued makeup man, whose eyes were wet with misery. "She threw us out. We didn't do anything wrong!"

"I didn't effen finish da hair!" wailed Petier, the Hungarian wig specialist, who, for reasons unclear to anyone, dressed like a seventeenth-century buccaneer.

Petier was as dedicated to hairpieces as a cardiac surgeon is to arteries, and George was king of the cosmetic queens. These were real professionals, masters of their craft, as experienced in the twentieth-century art of celebrity butt smooching as anyone on earth. What could possibly have gone wrong?

"I'm sure it was just a misunderstan—" I began, just in time to be interrupted by the trailer door being slammed open by a deranged five-foot-nine supermodel screaming at the top of her willowy lungs while pumping both slender fists angrily into the air. As all three of us simultaneously dropped to the ground to cover our vulnerable areas, Naomi's hair weave went flying into the distance.

"And don't ever fucking come back, you stupid fucking cunts!"
she spewed, her lipgloss smeared with bile.

"Oh . . . hi, Sharon darling. Didn't see you," Naomi said, greeting me in dulcet tones, before giving the stink-eye to George and
Petier and reslamming the door with a resounding *thwack!*

"*Hmmm.* Let me see what I can do." I trembled as I tentatively
entered the trailer of ultimate model hell.

Hearkening back to my many unpleasant experiences with
deeply schizoid media titans, I prepared to wield the most powerful tool in my celebrity handler kit, namely The Overkill Paradox
Steps (TOPS), which require the meticulous enactment of the following measures:

1. Pretend to listen carefully as the utterly crazy famous
   person delivers an entirely unreasonable rationalization of
   their completely indefensible behavior toward a totally
   innocent human victim.
2. Agree with the utterly crazy person that the totally
   innocent human victim *is* a complete asshole just for being
   alive.
3. Demonstrate great personal animus and unjustified animal
   rage toward the totally innocent human victim who has
   made the terrible mistake of just being alive.
4. Rant and make *more* dire physical threats toward the
   totally innocent human victim than the utterly crazy
   famous person has already made.
5. Continue until the utterly crazy person starts to think you
   are crazier than they are and starts to protect the victim
   out of a sense of propriety, or at least a sense of
   possessiveness.

It's important to remember that restoring harmony to genuine
psychotics requires a firm commitment to counterpsychosis, because if you don't mirror the exact level of ridiculous overentitle-

ment that started the whole mess in the first place, you'll just make things way worse. Unless your famous crazy person jumps the cuckoo gun, as Naomi was about to do, and actually begins expressing contriteness before you even get a chance to explain how appropriate it is to be so inappropriate.

"I'm really sorry, but I hate it when those douche bags start messing with my shit," Naomi stated by way of apology, batting her four-inch fake eyelashes at me like Olive Oyl.

Peace was restored to the Star Wagon as Petier returned to complete the glue gunning of large tufts of human hair to Naomi's skull while George messed with her shit by applying invisible foundation to Naomi's already flawless skin.

Now, as I finally locate Naomi over by the Peruvian village water fountain, I make a note to tell her to stop grinding her ten-thousand-dollar Gucci sandals into our imported Peruvian dirt clumps—that stuff is expensive. Meanwhile, she is sipping a diet beverage through a straw while garbed in a fashionista's interpretation of Peruvian village daily wear, which basically translates into half an ounce of muslin. The crew is deeply grateful.

"What's up, Naomi?" I ask when I get to the fountain, wishing I'd brought a step stool. By craning my neck I can almost see the bottom of her perfect chin, which rests at the end of her perfect throat, which rests at the top of her languid stems, which rest on the basin of the fountain that stands at least five feet away from the rest of her. A quick calculation confirms my suspicion that three-quarters of what is known as Naomi is actually her legs. This also confirms an earlier suspicion that I am a squat, Neanderthal Jewess.

"Sharon . . ." Naomi drawls in her broad British accent, "I'm just not getting it together with Michael, and I don't know what's going wrong. Herb said you could tell me what to do."

Omigod. This is a conspiracy. After promising his manager to make Michael look like "a real man," Herb has laid upon Naomi the Herculean task of imbuing Michael Jackson with heterosexual credibility for a song titled "In the Closet," and now Naomi is try-ing to shove it back on me.

"I don't know why, but Michael doesn't want to get next to me."

Du-uh. Michael and Naomi are supposed to be performing a sexy dance duet, but off-set or on, he won't come within five feet of her. It's like he hates her. Like a dog hates a cat. Like a cock-roach hates a shoe. Like a man hates a woman?

"Well, Naomi, obviously, he has issues. You've just got to get in there and go for it. You know, do your catwalk thing. Shimmy. Shake. Grab him. I mean, c'mon, you know how to work it."

I babble on. Like I know what she does on a catwalk. Like I know how to shimmy, shake, and work it. Like I know how to get Michael Jackson to grind his hips anywhere other than into thin air. Besides, why am I giving a supermodel lessons in how to initi-ate a carnal relationship? The last two men on her dance card were supposedly Mike Tyson and Robert De Niro. She probably knows more about tumescent arousal than Masters and Johnson put together. Then I accidentally say something of interest.

"Naomi, if in the end you can't count on Michael coming to you, maybe you should just think about going to him."

All of a sudden Naomi's face lights up, as if she has just heard the solution to *The Da Vinci Code*.

"Oooh. I know what to do. Thanks."

Ta-dum. Another problem solved. Check, check, and double-check. I have no idea what she's up to, and her sudden confidence makes me a little nervous, but on the other hand, I want to run right over and tell Herb that the problem is solved so he'll start shooting again.

"Great, Naomi. Keep up the good work!" I salute her as I walk away. Actually, she hasn't done any good work yet, but I want her to feel confident about making $20,000 a day, so that she can get Michael to sex it up with her, so we can start shooting, so we can finish shooting, so I can check the fuck out of my luxury hotel and go home.

On the other hand, I have to ask myself, what am I doing? Why do I care? What does it matter if Michael Jackson waits seven centuries to finish pretending to want to have sex with Naomi Campbell so it will look like he's half as straight as nobody believes he ever was in the first place? What strange demon pushes me to subdue chaos, suppress lassitude, and fight inaction on the part of others, even though it would profit me greatly not to do so?

As I thoughtlessly tread upon several heatstroked crew members, I consider that all I have to do is lie down in a pile of yak shit and I'll wake up one week later as a multizillionaire. Because the way this video has been set up, the more time we waste, the more money I make. Naturally, it took the combined genius of Michael Jackson's ten separate financial teams to come up with this system, which, as far as I know, stands alone as the best possible way to throw away money.

First, let me explain standard video procedure:

1. The record company and the production company arrive at the standard final agreed-upon script.
2. The standard final agreed-upon script is broken down so that it can be utilized to arrive at the standard final agreed-upon contract price.
3. This standard agreed-upon contract price is agreed upon, whereupon the standard agreed-upon production company fee is put into place.
4. The standard agreed-upon production company fee is agreed upon to be a standard 15 percent of the standard agreed-upon contract gross.

The only problem is that the standard gross costs aren't actually based on the actual gross but on the pretend gross, and my standard 15 percent would be more like 20 percent, but I'm not allowed to mention it, even though they already know. Why? Because it's the system. Unless I charge a 20 percent markup, I can't make any money, but if I tell them that I'm charging 20 percent, I can't get any jobs. This has been the model for the music video industry since its inception. My executive producer taught it to me, and I teach it to all of my executive producers, and they teach it to all of their producers. The record companies know all about it, and we all pretend that they don't, because the way they see it, if they don't let us charge a 20 percent markup, we'll just charge 25 percent instead.

On "In the Closet" we are not dealing directly with a record company, because Michael Jackson owns his own videos and has set up his own system, which has been designed to subvert the time-honored system of mutual duplicity that has been honed so carefully by record and production companies over the years. Nope, after weeks of talks and rounds of negotiations with the Michael Jackson legal and financial teams, we've agreed instead to a special MJJ Productions "cost plus" deal, in which we will be paid a straight 15 percent on whatever we actually spend, which will be determined by the actual bills.

Now the way this works out, the more nonfat tempeh cookies we eat, the more Tibetan yaks we milk, and the more dancing Aztecs we train to dance in the middle of a desert lakebed in the noonday sun, the more my price goes up. Simply put, for every dollar I spend on the video, I get fifteen cents to take home. For every $100,000 spent, I get $15,000. And so on.

Even though I wouldn't usually accept this kind of deal, I decide to roll with it, because based on talking to other production companies, I know that the gross is going to be *way* high. As it turns out, I have no idea how way high until we are actually shooting—or, more important, not shooting. Because this is not the right kind of deal for this kind of artist, who is, ironically, the only artist who can make this kind of deal.

If Michael Jackson decides not to come by the set because he has a headache or a nosebleed or a sunburn or food poisoning from eating the KFC chicken that he and his security team are covertly purchasing while they make the rest of us eat asparagus and millet from the good-karma caterers, the expense of holding over the cast, crew, and high-fiber food products is still being charged out at a 15 percent fee. Or, if Michael Jackson decides he needs ten thousand yo-yos to go to ten thousand goat herders who are hanging around a fake Peruvian village that has to be shipped into the Mojave Desert, that cost is still being totted up at 15 percent. Or if Michael Jackson wants to shut down production while he shares tea cookies with Red Buttons, I'm still getting my 15 percent. Or if certain people have certain liberties to talk to certain press people about how cool they are for two hours at a stretch while we have a full crew and the cast and a half of Noah's ark sitting around and chewing their cuds, well, I get 15 percent of that too.

Like I said, if I could only just lie back and enjoy it, I could walk out of these desert salt flats with enough cash to create an army of Sharon Orecks who look as much like me as the two exact photo doubles on our video—who are obliged to keep going out and getting the same cosmetic surgeries as Michael if they want to keep their jobs—look like him.

The longer this takes, the more the only person who wins here is me. I should just relax and let the asylum run its own show.

But this is where the professional and the personal meet up. Because I can pretend that my job is to assemble talent with finance and provide structure for creativity to flourish, but actually it is my function to re-create the world in less than seven days. I don't like to make money for nothing. I don't like wasting time and resources. I don't like staying in luxury hotels with top-notch body masseurs and tennis courts and swimming pools. Well, okay, so I do, but not with these folks.

Meanwhile, I go to sulk in my production trailer while Herb comes in to meet the latest creative director whom we've duped into writing the latest Levi's "Loose Interpretation" commercial concept, which Herb, of course, hates just as much as all the other ones.

"No! I just don't like it! This is not what I want!" he bleats, over and over.

Hildy, my commercial executive producer, who has just driven three hours to get here, starts clutching her heart as the creative dude hangs his head and I gird my loins for the usual suspects. Because it's Herb's particular style not to tell you what he wants and then to whine loudly when he hasn't gotten it, even though he couldn't tell you what he wanted in the first place so he wouldn't have to whine about it later.

As usual, I'm going to end up writing this concept, which will be exactly what all the other concepts have been on all of Herb's other videos and commercials: a herd of young hard-bodied guys and one or two lithe twenty-year-old girls running around half naked on a smooth, uniformly consistent white or black surface in the middle of the day in Hawaii, Malibu, or the Palm Desert salt flats. Blah blah blah.

The new creative writer, who is now the old creative writer, leaves the trailer, bent and defeated.

"Sharon, I don't want that! *You have to give me what I want!*" Herb yells at me.

"And what the hell is that anyway? This is the seventh script you've rejected, and they're all based on your own ideas. And stop yelling at me!"

Herb looks at me in complete shock.

"I am not yelling at you!" he yells.

Suddenly, a disgustingly explicit two-minute-long fart sound wafts from the trailer bathroom.

Herb immediately starts cracking up as his new boyfriend, who is currently being paid $400 a day to hold Herb's glasses case, comes out of the toilet and makes more fart sounds. They walk off into the distance, laughing hysterically.

Meanwhile, they actually start shooting something with Naomi and Michael over by the giant waterwheel and—hooray!—soon we have almost *one whole minute* of film in the can! Unfortunately, it's mostly shots of Naomi dancing over to Michael, who is frantically dancing as far away from her as he can get without being out of frame. Then we see Naomi pull Michael over for a confidential tête-à-tête, after which Michael literally leaps away from her grasp, runs away from the set, and disappears via his makeshift black corridor of night into his trailer.

A conference is promptly called for, and Herb is summoned to the trailer, from which he emerges, blinking at the bright sun as if in a daze.

"Sharon . . ." He calls me over.

"Yesssss?" I reply.

"What exactly did you tell Naomi to do earlier?"

I think very hard for a minute about what I actually told Naomi to do earlier.

"Nothing really, I just told her to dance closer to him. Why? What did he say?"

Herb cannot hold it in. His face is bright red. He pulls me in for a whisper.

"Michael said that Naomi asked him if she could, uh, uh, *suck his cock*."

"Oh my God," I say.

"He says he's never coming out of that trailer."

"Oh my God," I say again.

I look over at Naomi, who looks back at me with her eyes wide with fake innocence.

"What?" she says, knowing full well *exactly* what we are talking about.

Somehow, Herb manages to get Michael back on the set. Then, somehow, he manages to make it look like they're dancing with each other. Then Michael doesn't show up for the next day, so we all go back to the hotel and play tennis. Then he agrees to work the next day, on the condition that Naomi stays at the hotel and plays tennis. Then we shoot Michael dancing in silhouette and prancing in profile and slamming closet doors. Then we finish the video. We have to, because that night is *MTV's My Dinner with Michael,* an event for which hundreds of thousands of international competitors have been whittled down to the twenty-five lucky winners who've written the most heartfelt postcards outlining their reasons for wanting to have dinner with Michael Jackson.

They have been flown in from India and Japan and Brazil and the Soviet Union and Finland and Arizona and Hawaii and Australia because their whole life's desire is to travel for three days and three nights to drive out to the middle of nowhere, so they can be put up in a Holiday Inn with faulty plumbing and a broken air conditioner, picked up in an old school bus, and hauled out to break bread in a teepee in the desert with their hero, their idol, and their living deity, Mr. Michael Jackson, who is seriously thinking about not actually showing up at all.

Because even though MTV has spent millions of dollars, six months, blood, sweat, and tears in preparing for this event, Michael couldn't give a flying fuck through a rolling doughnut about the mammoth canvas circus tent or the thousands of calla lilies or the Baccarat crystal or the fine linens or the polished silver or the sword swallowers or the fire jugglers or the flautists and the bongo players and the people doing the boogie-woogie on top of a mound of burning-hot coals—not to mention the camels and llamas and elephants and pony rides and the large exotic birds of prey exhibit and the white tigers in a cage exhibit. Because what Michael cares about is the forty-seven children who were recently imported from a private school in Palm Desert to sing welcome songs to Michael so that he will actually show up and get out of his armored car.

"Sharon, we need at least fifty singing kids, otherwise Michael won't show up on time," Abbey, the extremely tense head of MTV talent, had begged me earlier that afternoon. "He says he doesn't want to come, because he doesn't want to be around grown-ups, because he says they're boring."

The dinner has prompted a lot of bitter, frenzied, last-second dealings between Michael and MTV, who have already been blackmailed into promoting Michael from the "King of Pop" to the "King of Pop *and* Rock" by the threat that he wouldn't show up at this dinner at all. Now he is demanding at least four dozen warbling youngsters to show up for appetizers.

"Are you crazy? We're in the middle of a salt flat in the middle of the desert, forty miles from the nearest town. Where am I gonna get singing kids?"

At that exact moment, my excruciatingly adorable two-year-old daughter walks by in her little sailor dress and tiny gold John Lennon glasses singing Joni Mitchell's "Morning Morgantown" at the top of her squeaky little lungs.

I cut Abbey off before he has a chance to speak.

"Don't even. That one is *mine* and is currently unavailable for your MTV promotional needs. Get your own kids."

Of course, this is long before the rumors had turned into multimillion-dollar settlements and court cases, so it wasn't as sinister as it seems now. Meanwhile, as the sun set and the moon rose over the *My Dinner with Michael* tent, I was riding an elephant with my little girl when I saw Herb making an entrance past the paparazzi with Naomi, who appeared to be ten sheets to the wind at least forty paces before she even got to the bar.

"Naomi! Herb!" the photographers shouted as Herb attempted to steer Naomi down the red carpet. "How's the video?"

"I want to suck Michael Jackson's cock!" Naomi dutifully tried to inform the free press as Herb shoved her in the door while attempting to gag her with his spare hand.

Michael showed up two hours later to try the baba ghanoush, after which he shared pita triangles with his fans, who were barking like coyotes while they tried to stroke him. The subsequent publicity photos in *Rolling Stone* portray me clutching my adorable two-year-old daughter while she is dancing in her charming sailor dress in front of a dining table at which Michael Jackson sits in his black-and-red fake lieutenant's jacket, rigid and terrified, looking a lot like a cosmetically altered deer in the headlights as he tries to physically distance himself as much as possible from his tear-streaked fans, who include a fire juggler and two chicks wearing fruit on their heads leaning to get in the picture.

15

Work to Do

t's 1978, and, looking to advance my position, I graduated from being a vague assistant on a ridiculous, cheap movie to being a *specific* assistant on a shoddy, dumb movie where, as a second assistant film editor, I immediately increased my salary by 1,000 percent, even though I had zero experience and a bad attitude and had never slept with the producer. I probably do not need to mention that the producer looked like something that comes out of a can. I also probably do not need to mention that 1,000 percent more than twenty-five bucks is still not very much, especially minus tax.

My second movie purported to reveal the vast left-wing conspiracy behind the evil Bureau of Land Management, which was attempting to stymie the American way of life by preventing jackbooted American bikers from slaughtering the precious endangered baby animals that live on sacred Indian hunting grounds as they raced their motorbikes from Mexico to Canada.

Well, that's what the poster said. In reality, my second movie made less sense than the first movie, which made no sense at all. At least, that's what my grandma Rose said when I dragged her down to the big premiere at the Cineplex 6000, right behind Antonio's Burrito Barn on Vermont and Lincoln, where *Breaker! Breaker!* was double-billed with *It's Alive!*—the story of a bad baby who escapes his mother's uterus in order to become the first neo-natal serial killer.

"Vhy did you make dis?" Grandma inquired, striking me in the head with her clutch bag. "Vhy don't you make a nice pictchah, vit nice music?"

The last movie Grandma Rose had liked was *Song of Norway* (in Cinerama!), but this one, she emphasized with a stroke of her pocketbook, "vas a real *frassk* in de *pisk!*"

Grandma Rose was right. These movies *were* venal, puerile, and a big, giant slap in *der punim.* But if somebody was stupid enough to watch this shit, then why shouldn't I be stupid enough to earn from this shit?

Besides, the great thing about *The Great Ride* was that the production company had elected to shoot it in Canada, where they could mow down old timber, scatter endangered moose herds, and squish internationally protected Gila monsters at a great ex-change rate. The location shoot left me and the editing team hap-pily "home alone," working by ourselves in the cheapest editing facility in East Hollywood, the back rooms of Producers' Sound Services, a sound effects house on Santa Monica Boulevard that had been providing the film industry with squeaks, bow-wows, and thank-ya-ma'ams since 1943.

Tucked away between boxes of gunshots and rolls of car screeches and crates of donkey brays, I would retreat to do my assisting in between hot dogs at Pink's, combination platters at Los Burritos, and strips of chicken and eggs at Teriyaki Lola's. In my salad days, I rarely went without eight squares per day, in the form of breakfast, brunch, snunch, lunch, snee, tea, sninner, din-ner, snupper, supper, and a midnight snack. This is when I learned that when you are profoundly bored, even three packs of Marl-boros per day will not stanch your ravenous need for immediate gratification.

Still there was something about putting things in their proper place that satisfied the chaos subduer deep inside me. Taking a great big mess and turning it into a teeny tiny mess sang to me with the same kind of silent scouring power as a sixteen-ounce bottle of Mr. Clean. I liked to keep things tidy.

After all, I was a mommy. A done-in, pooped-out, dog-tired mommy, to be exact. Although my parents had accepted me back in the family, they still hewed to their "keep your personal problems to yourself" policy, leaving me to carve my own way in the world with full-time work, which had proved almost as unfulfilling as full-time welfare, although I had at least moved on to metaphorical streams of urine on my person. Luckily, Josh completely ignored the statistics on neglected children of single working mothers and turned out to be brilliant, loving, and self-motivated. On the other hand, since he was six and had started primary school, I had to look at child care options that dealt with the tricky hours between 3:00 and 6:00 p.m.

As it turned out, the identifying traits for child care specialists who fell within my financial constraints included constant foot tapping, rapid eye twitching, and lifelong addictions to inexpensive appetite suppressants. I finally found a decent service that would pick Josh up at school and play with him until 7:00 p.m., after which they started charging something bad, like a hundred dollars every ten minutes. I stuck with them for seven years, until the new personnel director asked me if I knew anybody who wanted to buy some coke.

Bye-bye, day care; hello, latchkey.

Meanwhile, as soon as the production phase of the movie was over and the director came home, I was promptly fired. Apparently, our leader did not appreciate my remarks regarding the nontherapeutic usage of medical-grade laughing gas. On the other hand, he could have been really annoyed that I accidentally threw a very small amount of motion picture negative into the big green trash bin because I thought it was a box of pizza.

An interesting note: The film's editor proved himself too talented, good-looking, and efficient to get himself shit-canned, so he was forced to finish the movie and get a credit. This strange pattern would repeat itself for many years, until he got so rich and famous that he was forced to live happily ever after.

I, however, went on to be fired from a vast number of appalling trailer-trash movies spanning a vast assortment of appalling trailer-trash genres, with the only exception being hardcore porn. After mistakenly attending the Hollywood Masquers Erotic Film Festival of 1977 with what turned out to be my gay date, I have been unable to walk through a Ralph's produce department without experiencing severe anxiety upon sighting a Japanese eggplant. Once, however, while I was syncing dailies for *Dribble*, a dismal musical comedy about women in basketball, I *did* manage to secure an editing position for my dear friend Margaret on the science fiction sex movie being cut in the room next door to me.

Nudes on Uranus, the editor assured me, "is not in *any way* pornography, because it actually has a plot."

"Well, I suppose that's true . . ." Margaret mused uncertainly after looking at the footage. "You're not exactly positive the minute you see the characters how they're going to have sex, so I guess it's more of a mystery."

Meanwhile, due to budget constraints and scheduling conflicts, and because he still didn't trust me not to spill Diet Dr Pepper all over the film negative, my old editor refused to hire me again as a second assistant editor. As a personal favor, however, he agreed to hire me as a third assistant editor on his fourth movie.

"Make me a cup of coffee, will you, dear?" asked the big fat executive producer on the first long, dull day, with the clear understanding that he was not actually asking and that I was not really a dear.

"Can I offer you some artificial sugar and powdered milk with that?" I immediately replied, before running out to get fresh water and granules for the coffeepot. In those bleak, pre-Starbucks years, café lattes with frothy low-fat milk in a patent-pending cup were still science fiction beverages from a far-off future, so you had to make the shit yourself.

As I began to shovel a fresh supply of Chock full o'Nuts into the coffee brewer, however, Danny, the first assistant on the movie, gave me the best piece of professional advice I have ever received.

"*Pssst . . .*" he whispered. "Put fourteen servings of coffee in that pot."

"Whaaaat?" I whispered back. "You're only supposed to put in six. It'll be, like, mud."

"Yeah." He nodded. "Or did you want him to ask you to do it again?"

Hmmmmm. Devious. Underhanded. Scheming. Subversive. I liked it. Shoveling fourteen scoops into the basket, plus one extra for luck, I stood back and hit the on button. Voilà—seven minutes later—volcanic sludge.

"Here you go, sir," I offered, handing over the cup-o-muck.

For what was probably the last time in his life, the executive producer sipped without looking and promptly responded with a satisfying gagging sound.

"*Eh eh eh ehe hehe,*" he choked as my special brew made its way past his esophageal reflex. "That is the single worst substance I have ever poured down my throat!"

"Oh gosh, sir, I am sooo sorry," I exulted. "I made it myself, just the way I *always* do. Let me go back and try again."

"*No!*" the executive producer replied, getting away from me as quickly as possible. "I'll get my own, thanks."

"Old army trick," said Danny modestly. "Works every time."

With these kind of labor-saving strategies, I was soon able to accomplish a little bit more than nothing, which was apparently all I needed to do to convince the writer of the movie that I was finally ready to start producing. Thus I made my debut as producer on *The Door Man*, a postfeminist ten-minute horror film about a young woman who is denied entrance to her own building by her psychotic doorman until she is forced to bludgeon him to death with an ax.

More important, I had only $3,000 and three weeks to slap together the cast, a crew, and four locations. I'm almost sure that in all the rush I did not lie and offer to pay people actual money for actual work, just as I'm practically positive that I didn't promise anyone my first-born infant, because he was already eight.

Then, with a week to go until our shoot day, the weird Scandinavian dude whose name I could never pronounce, let alone spell, suddenly dropped out of being the gaffer (guy in charge of lights), citing "complicated, unforeseen personal commitments." Close personal scrutiny of Doorgen Boorgen Guurgin's three-buildings-south-of-my-best-friend-Margaret-Goldsmith's-duplex apartment would reveal his "complicated, unforeseen commitments" to include drinking hard liquor, screwing his punk rock girlfriend, and smoking a giant Pakistani bong.

Which is why, after my traumatic experience with the foreign, scary-named first gaffer, I was looking for a brusque, all-American type, or at least somebody whose name had fewer than eighteen vowels and who was willing to work for free. As if in answer to my prayers, I immediately got a phone call from a guy named Bill, who had just moved to town from New York and wanted to "network."

"Well, maybe you should network with me . . ." I suggested huskily. After all, there was a one-in-a-million chance that he might actually be a cute straight guy who wasn't a total lying scumbag with hair all over his hunchback.

"Well, okay!" he replied gamely. After all, there was a one-in-a-million chance that I might be an attractive chick who wasn't a huge bitch with open herpes sores on my cankles. "But you'll have to pick me up, because my car just blew up."

"No problem." I continued lying, burdening our new relationship with a dark secret about my vehicle. The truth was, my car had just blown a gasket and I was too poor to get it fixed.

I borrowed the director's car to go pick up the gaffer, who turned out to be a total babe wearing a red-and-white striped Brooks Brothers shirt with perfectly pressed blue jeans and bright white Converse tennis shoes. My first thought was, Holy God! That guy's a hottie!

My second thought was, Holy shit! That guy's a homo!

Disappointed but accepting, I loaded up the gay dude and drove him to our first location scout at a punk rock club on La Brea, where I had recently seen the Weirdos, the Go-Go's, and Joanna Went, a performance artist who liked to defile plush toys by rolling them in fake excrement.

At least I hope it was fake.

On the way there, Bill managed to drop several references to a couple of ex-girlfriends, leading me to believe he did not prefer the love that dare not speak its name except in Hollywood, New York, and most parts of Amsterdam. Hallelujah. By the time we got to Blackie's, I was smitten.

Unfortunately, I wasn't the only one.

"We're going to need a couple of extras in the bar scene who are sort of making out!" the director casually dropped.

"I'll do it with the new gaffer!" piped up the assistant director, Lizzie.

"Me too!" The camera assistant seconded the motion.

"I'm available," said my good friend Jane.

"I can help!" said the makeup guy.

"I can always do it myself!" said the director.

"I'm sorry, but none of you can make out with the new gaffer," I interjected quickly. "Bill is far too busy with all of his other unpaid duties to have sex with all of you."

Charmingly, Bill appeared to be oblivious, which made him even more attractive or, if I wanted to be paranoid, even more gay.

Finally, after much sturm und drang, we shot the whole movie in ten days. Every day, my crush got worse. But nine days into shooting, Bill still hadn't made a move.

Then, on the last day of shooting, Bill volunteered to "tie into" the fuse box of a huge apartment complex, thereby saving me the cost of renting a generator. If he were unsuccessful, it would sear his frontal lobe, electrocute his testicles, and fry his spinal column from the inside out. On the other hand, it would save me two hundred dollars!

"Are you sure you won't, er, injure yourself?" I asked, deeply conflicted. If Bill broiled his scrotum, I would never get a chance to love him, marry him, and have his children. Then again, I *really* couldn't afford that generator.

"Probably not," Bill answered thoughtfully. "Once, in New York, when I tied directly into the subway system, I blacked out for an hour, but I didn't *die*."

That did it. There was no way I was microwaving a supposed straight guy to save somebody else's money.

"You know what?" I said. "I think I'll call the generator place."

Then, while I was on the phone to the equipment house, Bill disappeared, only to return ten minutes later with his hair raised two inches above his scalp, smelling comfortingly of burnt toast.

"Fixed," he said proudly, rubbing his blackened palms together.

Thanks to Bill's noble sacrifice, his brain was rebooted and he remembered to ask me on a date. Unfortunately I couldn't go until I got a babysitter, but I informed the entire crew of our upcoming love affair, just so that none of the girls would try any of their tricks.

Two weeks later, we went out to dinner and he accidentally forgot his wallet. Then he told me he was in love with me but had inadvertently slept with my best friend. Then I inadvertently backed my Plymouth Capri into his Volkswagen Squareback and told him I loved him too. Then he got evicted from his apartment, so he moved into mine.

He has not moved out since.

It has been twenty-six years. Someday we are going to clear him a closet.

16

Loose Interpretation

'd like to state for the record that I did not *mean* to make millions of dollars producing dumb-ass television commercials.
Let me explain.

Back in the nineties, a company I'll call the Great Big Beer Corporation contracted my company to do a series of multimillion-dollar commercials for a brand new product called "ice beer."

"So . . ." I asked the brand manager the first day, squinting at the six-inch gleaming beverage cans being lit by an Academy Award–winning director of photography with two billion watts of blue-tinted lights that would better enhance its "iciness."

"What exactly *is* ice beer anyway?"

"Er, uh, well . . ." He twitched, nervously scanning the horizon for regulatory agencies. "Actually, ice beer is exactly like regular beer, in that it *is* regular beer, except that it is *called* ice beer."

"I see!" I said, not at all surprised to find him addled, conflicted, and paranoid.

Commercial types regularly knock back large buckets of 100 percent grain alcohol with their Zoloft, Paxil, Ritalin, crystal meth, and quaaludes, so they often get short-tempered and start hallucinating. I get short-tempered and start hallucinating too, but only when I'm right and everybody else is wrong, which it turns out is not exactly all the time.

"Well . . ." I foolishly blundered on, "then why don't you just spend millions of dollars selling regular beer and forget about selling 'ice beer,' since it doesn't really exist?"

The brand manager winced in horror. Was it possible that his company had given millions of advertising dollars to someone who had failed to grasp the basic principles of the politics of desire? Was I unaware that a corporation was obliged to its plenary stockholders to pretend that its product had an actual market value? Did I somehow suppose that the average drinker of light alcoholic drinks wished to be left unmolested by sophisticated media campaigns, to have to go figure out his beverage preferences all by himself?

"As I am very sure you know, Sharon," the brand manager sternly lectured me, "today's beverage consumer is no longer *brand loyal*. This means that our customers cannot be relied upon to drink Great Big Beers instead of Really Gigantic Beers, even though they're both exactly the same as all other beers, except more expensive!"

Here, the brand manager paused to tic into space, his heart clearly aching for those heady salad days when loyal consumers chugged Great Big Beers by the truckload, regardless of price, product design, or disgusting urinelike aftertaste.

"Unfortunately," he continued, his eyes now spinning like lotto balls, "in order to survive in today's crazy competitive market, we have been forced to provide our old customers with a new product, which is exactly the same as the old product, but which costs more, so that consumers will want to come back to the old product, after they've spent more money on the same thing with an unpleasant metallic twang!"

I'd like to believe that I made this conversation up, but then I'd have to be delusional as well as paranoid, and my unconventional therapist, Dr. Hannah S. Brinker, says that's way worse. Meanwhile, just so you know, there is no such thing as "ice beer"— except in Canada, where reality, like so many vowel sounds, is annoyingly different. There, regular beer is frozen and the ice crystals removed, increasing the alcohol content from 5 to 14 percent.

Of course, you aren't allowed to market beer in America if it is actually whiskey, because that would be *fake advertising*, which is not the same as *false advertising*, and let me explain exactly why I'm not lying.

Originally we were approached by a big Chicago agency to come up with a multimillion-dollar ad scenario in which an internationally renowned action-movie star would do violent battle with a despotic villain who is bent on the destruction of a universe that is full of scantily clad babes who partake in fake sports activities that could indirectly encourage bored beer drinkers to try a new alcoholic pseudoproduct at their next Super Bowl. As is pro forma with the commercial process, a conference call was set up so that all parties could get together to lie, flatter, and kiss one another's butts without sneers, snarls, and fuck-you hand signals being detected.

"Go wild! Be weird! Get as arty and punk rock and wacky European-style crazy as you want!" the agency promised, to the ecstasy of my emotionally inconstant bald French director, who immediately began to rifle though his "creative diary" for the Francis Bacon electric chair rip-off scenario sketches that he had been unable to sell to the Taco Bell people the previous week. "All you need are those four elements!"

"Why can't we just use a real sport?" I asked with my usual lack of advertising savvy, as my snotty French director, who could barely be bothered to get up in the morning for less than two hundred grand and a café au lait machine from Paris, stared at me with his usual disdain.

"Because zere is no real sport in Americas, because zey play ze stupid ballfoot instead of soccer!" he muttered off-speaker, to the titters of his loyal French assistant, whose main job was to snigger at anti-American humor while vigorously picking his nose.

"According to the advertising and marketing code of the Beer

Institute of America," the producer explained, "we cannot depict a positive relationship between real beer and real sports, because then we would be unofficially encouraging people to get drunk on liquor during football games."

"But you *are* encouraging people to get drunk during football games," my brain accidentally disgorged.

"No we're not. We're encouraging people to drink a refreshing, light alcoholic beverage that just might be around when they're already watching football, but we wouldn't know about that, would we?"

In truth, the alcohol industry self-instituted a ban on hard liquor advertising in the eighties and nineties, just to keep the government from stepping in and doing it themselves. Luckily, this barbaric restriction was (self-) lifted in 2004, right after the Bush administration made it clear to the world that there was nothing more unpatriotic than business regulations, including drunkenness, death, and (financial) depression.

Meanwhile, we got the ice beer job, mostly because our main competition used his conference call to identify the head of creative affairs as a "stupid fucking idiot."

"I may be stupid," the agency producer told us, "but not stupid enough to work with somebody who calls me a fucking idiot."

Unfortunately, he didn't feel so smart at the end of the job, when the Great Big Beer distributors of America got together to watch our punk rock, arty, Felliniesque ice beer commercial.

"Can't you just give us what we want for two fucking million dollars?" the stupid agency producer had yelled at the snotty French director, after he refused for the third straight time to dress the women fake athletes in pretty pink-flowered string bikinis instead of black vinyl dominatrix corsets.

"Merde! You are *très blahblahblahblah!*" replied the director in his native language, which thankfully nobody was around to properly translate, or they would've gone back to the original director, who had called them "fucking idiots" in the first place.

Meanwhile, although this job had many, many low points, the absolute lowest arrived when the agency producer returned to a tense preproduction meeting following a brief trip to the O Pictures unisex bathroom.

"Hey, Sharon!" he yelled, interrupting the meeting. "Guess what? There's some shit on the floor in there!"

Naturally I assumed he was kidding. I mean, how often do you find a pile of steaming excrement somewhere it's not supposed to be?

Okay. I take that back.

The agency producer escorted me to the doorway of the bathroom, where we both stood, awestruck, as he carefully pointed out a neat, amoeba-shaped piece of poop sitting quietly atop the shining gray tile conveniently located adjacent to our capacious new Italian-designed toilet.

"*Eeeeeeeeeeewwwwwwwwwww!*" I screamed. "Lynn! Hildy! Joanne! Somebody get in here! There's a turd on the floor!"

After Lynn, Hildy, every single member of our office staff, and the freelance cleaning crew refused point-blank to pick up the doody, I at last understood the true meaning of being the boss.

"I'm gonna give you all one last chance to do the right thing—who pooped on the floor?" I called out to the office. Receiving no reply, I held my nose and swooped in to do the deed, depositing the mystery log in the Italian-designed porcelain bowl, where it was flushed away forever, along with all my hopes for a life of dignity.

Because as you might have guessed by now, I never meant to make commercials. My career trajectory, in my mind, included working with great artists who would heal the world with their brilliant visions and iconoclastic voices. Unfortunately, it was the eighties, the era of yuppies, Ray-Bans, and Ronald Reagan, under whose all-encompassing lack of ethical leadership the old-fashioned sins of greed, selfishness, and narcissism had been reconfigured as new-fashioned American values.

By 1985, the economy was up, God was back, and MTV had become the "it" channel, thanks to the spoiled-rotten American teenager, who had recently graduated from national moral threat to national role model. Suddenly, everybody on the rapidly de-greening earth wanted to act, look, and consume like a fifteen-year-old by snatching up the Twix bars, Noxzema creams, and Nike sports shoes that were being marketed on MTV.

As it became obvious that any association with the music tele-vision lifestyle led to a direct increase in retail sales, the squaresville buttoned-down, serge-suited advertising con men of the type formerly featured in *Bewitched* episodes were forced to rethink themselves as stylish metrosexuals sporting baggy Levi's, soul patches, and leather pants, courting the self-conscious grooviness of us MTV people with money, money, and more money.

Somehow I managed to avoid all this hullabaloo until the very late eighties, when I hooked up with the director Herb Ritts, who came to me with a series of spots for which he had been recommended with Calvin Klein Enterprises. Setting up the tra-ditional commercial conference call, we all made ourselves com-fortable for what turned out to be an hour and a half of the usual bullshit.

"Escape is a sexy, stylish blend of herbs and flowers, intended to suggest the sexy, elegant style of Calvin's sexy, elegant wife, Kelly, whose interests include horses, pools, and being rich," ex-plained the agency art director.

"Omigod!" exclaimed Herb. "I *love* Kelly!"

"Omigod!" exclaimed the agency producer. "Kelly loves *you*!"

"Omigod!" exlaimed Herb. "I *love* swimming!"

"Omigod!" exclaimed the agency producer. "*We* love swim-ming!"

"Omigod!" I exclaimed. "I thought Calvin Klein was married to John Travolta."

A recent article on Studio 54 floated past my mind's eye, fea-turing Calvin's tanned masculine features leering at a go-go boy in a gold lamé banana hammock who looked to be shoving a capsule of amyl nitrate into his left nostril.

"Shut up, you lame-ass!" hissed my executive producer, Hildy, shoving her fist into the speakerphone. "As usual you have everything wrong! That was David Geffen!"

Hildy was perpetually on edge about my lack of advertising savvy, which she correctly assumed could cost her valuable Christmas bonuses, unlimited access to fine alcohol and drugs, and free plane tickets to sunny island locations.

"Say you're sorry!" she whispered.

"I'm sorry," I said. "What I meant to say was: Calvin Klein is clearly quite masculine, as is clear from his fine underwear line."

"Your concept should include a horse and a pool," the agency producer continued, completely ignoring me, "and sexy young people like Calvin and Kelly who look hot, hunky, hetero, and happily married."

"Great!" said Herb. "Oh. I would like it to be *very* cinematic."

"Cinematic," in advertising parlance, means "suggestive of big Academy Award–winning movies"—as in, sweeping helicopter shots, complex crane moves, and classy, slow-motion body groping.

"Great!" said the agency producer.

"Great!" said Herb. "I'll think of something great! We'll get great actors! We'll get great places! I'll write a great treatment! We'll have great cinematography! It'll be great!"

Although Herb made millions of dollars, he never employed an adjective other than "great." Meanwhile, six weeks and fifteen fired writers later, Herb summoned me home from Easter vacation to write a treatment myself.

"I hate these!" Herb pouted, tossing all the concepts to the floor, including every conceivable plot possibility involving water, saddles, and being young, in love, and egregiously wealthy. "They're not great! They should be great!"

"What are you yelling about now?" I asked, annoyed. My

aborted vacation at Canyon Ranch had cost me at least one-eighth of a pound, not to mention a basic grounding in square-dance aerobics.

"I'm not yelling!" Herb screamed. "Just don't give me what I don't want! Just make it great!"

Two hours later, I handed Herb a two-page shot list that was glistening with beads of perspiration, rippling with toned deltoid muscles, and tightly packed inside a slightly used pair of two-sizes-too-small ball-cupping tighty whities. Voilà! Greatness achieved!

"It's great!" said Herb.

"It's brilliant!" said the creative director.

"It's genius!" cried Mr. Klein.

"A million four?" said the account manager in our next conference call. "Doesn't that seem a little high to you for a couple of days' shooting?"

"Jesus!" I snorted indignantly. "What dumb-ass would say it would cost a million four! All we're doing is shooting half-naked teenagers skipping around on salt flats for three hours a day!"

"You're the big dumb-ass, you big dumb-ass!" Hildy hissed at me disrespectfully, while jamming her fist once again into the conference speaker. "Look at the fucking budget! You signed it yourself!"

"Er, uh, ehhhh . . ." I was forced to uncomfortably reverse myself. "What I mean is, we've got an internationally renowned photographer, two hundred scantily clad supermodels, their assistants, their assistants' assistants, seven million feet of film, and protected state park land! We've had to cut our mark up to less than zero percent just to shoot night and day for two solid weeks!"

On that one occasion I made more money than I had ever made in my entire professional life put together. Thus the greed seed was planted, as agencies started calling around the clock.

"Careful product testing has proven conclusively that our credit card consumers want rich celebrities telling them how to save money while standing in front of a backlit projection of the writhing cosmos," agency producers would say when I picked up the phone. "How would your director best go about showing this?"

"Hmmm . . ." I would pretend to think, my mind drifting off to a pleasantly suggestive French-language brain-movie starring me and Johnny Depp. The commercial process was so unmitigatedly boring that I just assumed I was putting in a day's work by *pretending* to give a shit. Unfortunately, people in advertising expect you not just to pretend bad shit is good shit, but also to pretend old shit is new shit, and more shit is better shit. In this crazy, cockeyed caravan, the *correct advertising response* is to repeat back exactly what has already been said to you, only with a different number of syllables.

Yessss. A trusted archetype of some renown . . . I was supposed to respond. *Perhaps the talented Ms. Barbra Streisand, President Jimmy Carter, or . . . Cher, wearing sensible shoes and a dark brown wig, discussing the democratic principles of good credit with the primordial universal miasma pulsating behind her, suggesting wealth, prosperity, and the limitless possibilities for eternal shopping!*

"Duh!" would go my Tourette's-ish bad-advertising response instead. "Why don't you just stick a rich movie star in front of a background projection of a writhing cosmos and I'll bring the fucking doughnuts?"

"Barbarian!" the agency producers would snipe at me in horror. My halfhearted attempts at bold, illusion-busting openness were a slap in the face to the marketing professionals who had spent six years at Ivy League colleges so they could hone their degrees, get a job, and trick people into buying shit they didn't need with money they didn't have. The fact is, the people who create advertising feel a deep fear of those who *buy* advertising, because they can't believe they're going to get away with it forever. I mean, isn't anybody going to stop them? Won't somebody get pissed? Isn't there a law against lying? Isn't God opposed?

Although I produced commercials from 1986 to 1997, the na-

dir of my entire career occurred during the Levi's "Loose Interpretation" commercial series, which took place in the summer of
1991, on all the islands of Hawaii. It was the last job I did with
Herb Ritts, and it was the worst production of my entire life, from
day one, when Herb called me to say that I needed to call his
friend Bobby, who was the line producer for the biggest, meanest commercial director in the whole world, who had recently
managed to lose his long-standing directorship of the Levi's account by calling the creative director a "dumb fucking retard!"

"I may be dumb," the creative director had said, "but not dumb
enough to work with somebody who calls me a fucking retard."

No, you're not crazy. You did just read the same story five and
a half pages ago. The advertising business is built on reducing life
to thirty-second spots, so there is a lot of what they like to call
"same old."

Meanwhile, Bobby had suggested to the fucking retard creative director that they should try working with his old friend
Herb Ritts, who never uttered a discouraging word, since the only
adjective he employed was "Great!" In return for this "sugges-
tion," Bobby told me that the agency had "suggested" that he
ought to be compensated as a "rep," which he "suggested" ought
to be to the tune of about $60,000, which he "suggested" should
come off the top with no taxes taken out.

Beginning on this high note, a production meeting was called
at a Russian Hill steak house in San Francisco with the creative
director and his female art director, who consumed five Black
Russians apiece before tucking into a sixteen-ounce T-bone with
baked potato and butter, plus some fine French wines.

"We firmly believe in the value of red meat, tobacco, and
vodka," said the creative director, who looked as if he had just
completed six or seven life terms in a Siberian gulag.

"Yes . . ." agreed Leslie, his bottle-blonde consort, who'd (allegedly) been (recently) upgraded from secretary to agency art
director after the creative director had left his wife and children

to devote his life to animal fat. "What is the point in holding back?"

The creative director nodded at her dumbly, right as his nose spontaneously began to gush blood, which it continued to do for the next half hour for no apparent reason. According to rumor, the art director had literally fucked the creative director's brains out, until all that was left was a meat-eating man-puppet.

A napkin was stuffed inside the creative director's nostril right before Hildy, my old video executive producer, who had recently been promoted to become the new commercial executive producer, spilled an entire bottle of Châteauneuf-du-Pape all over the art director's white angora sweater, and then tried to wipe it off with her fingers.

Mysteriously, we were told the next day that we still had the job, although the art director demanded that we:

1. Shoot near five-star accommodations with sauna and pool.
2. Shoot in an exotic location with attractive local peoples.
3. Hire an attractive ex–male model named Boopsie as a special assistant and driver for the art director.
4. Hire another ex–male model to be the special assistant to the special assistant, because Boopsie didn't actually drive.
5. Pay Bobby $60,000 without a receipt.

Then, as we were prepping the job, Herb's accountant began calling me at least three times a day to demand a 50 percent share of all O Pictures profits.

"Don't do it!" hissed Hildy. "He's already making fifty grand a day, and we have to do seventy-five percent of all his work!"

It was true that Herb appeared to do absolutely nothing while O Pictures had become his own private factory. I wrote the ideas, Hildy did all the locations and casting, and teams of hundreds catered to his every whim. Meanwhile, his demands were growing;

the daily fees got bigger, the hotel rooms got more capacious, and we were all expected to be on call twenty-four hours a day just in case Herb came up with an idea, usually about where to book him a paid vacation in the middle of the shoot.

Then we got to the five-star resort hotel in Kona, Hawaii, where Bobby showed up to party with the agency and the actors, models, and spokespersons, who were all trashing their hotel rooms while drunk and stoned on cocaine, quaaludes, and black beauties. By the second day of the shoot, a silent war had been declared, as it became clear that Herb had formed a cabal with Bobby and the agency and their legions of highly paid bisexual party assistants.

Whatever. After four days in Sodom, all I wanted to do was go home and never see any of those crazy people ever again. It was crystal clear that this was not my world. Thank God.

Two weeks later, during a sales trip to Milan, I received a long-distance phone call from Herb.

"Sharon, I have made a decision, er, *whisper whisper* . . . I mean, a choice, that I will, er . . . work with another production company for commercials, because they have offered me a lot of mo . . . *whisper whisper*, I mean, an extraordinary opportunity, to work on, er, stuff, and I can't turn that down *whisper whisper*, I mean walk away, from this unique opportunity. In the meantime, we can still do videos together."

"Fuck you, Herb. You're a prick, you're a liar, and you told me last week that you were more loyal to me than to your own mother."

"*Whisper whisper* . . . I think I can validate your feelings *whisper whisper* on that issue.*"

"Herb, who the fuck is feeding you this psychobabble?"

At this, pandemonium broke loose on the other end of the line. I could actually hear the sound of somebody running away from the phone, as if I might reach through the line and start punching.

"This is not babble!" Herb replied after a long pause. "Er, I'll call you later."

Later that afternoon I received a phone message at the hotel, formally severing our relationship.

Et tu, Herb-e?

Bobby formed a company with Herb Ritts that stayed in business until Herb died in 2002. I never spoke to him again, although he did send me an autographed copy of his next book. We had a complicated, fractious relationship that was finally destroyed by the struggle for power and money. I miss him. I heard that Bobby moved to Morocco, where he abandoned his "bisexual identification" by moving in with his cute younger boyfriend.

I heard that the emotionally inconstant bald French director is still bald and French, and that he moved to the south of France with this cute younger girlfriend.

I don't know what happened to his nose-picker assistant.

The Great Big Beer agency producer who found the mystery shit became a big commercial director.

The mystery shitter has never been identified.

The (Nineteen) Sacred Steps Leading to Making a Rock Video

1. The recording artist makes a recording. Then he turns it in to the record company president. Then, the record company president doesn't listen to it.

2. The record company president dispenses the recording to his executive vice presidents, who pass it on to their senior vice presidents, who disseminate it among their managers, coordinators, and administrative assistants. Then they all don't listen to it either.

3. A consensus is arrived at. Everybody who didn't listen to the recording agrees that it is the best recording ever made. The recording artist concurs.

4. Everyone who has not listened to the recording gets together to tell the record company video department which unheard track is best, what the inexplicable lyrics mean, and why that song would make a good video.

5. The record company video department pretends to give a shit.

6. The record company video department picks ten video directors to approach with the track. Then they decide on a reasonable budget. Then they cut it in half.

7. The production company representative is approached by the record company representative, who explains what the lyrics are, what they really mean, and whom the artist is fucking. The production company pretends to be far too successful to care about such matters, except for the part about the fucking.

8. The production company tells the record company that the video director they are interested in is so talented and busy and cool that he just might be too exhausted

to work for lots of money. The record company
representative ignores this obvious lie.

9. The record company representative tells the production
company *exactly* how much money they want to spend.
He has automatically subtracted 20 percent from the
real amount, because he knows how production
companies are.

10. The production company representative tells the record
company representative that they will do the video for
exactly what they want to spend. In his head, he has
already added 40 percent, because he knows how record
companies are.

11. Directors submit little scripts called "concepts" that
reveal the deep inner subtext of the track. No one is
surprised that the song is a lot more profound than it
immediately appears and that its visual expression will
demand a lot of close-ups requiring lots of highly paid
cosmetics professionals.

12. The record company sends the best concepts to the
artist and advises him on who they think should do the
video. The artist tells the record company that it is a
stupid, fucked-up corporation that is not the boss of him
and that the artist himself will do the video. If the artist
sells at least ten million records, this tactic succeeds.
Otherwise the record company tells the artist how much
they respect him right before they totally ignore the shit
out of him and hire whomever they suggested in the first
place.

13. The production company producer draws up a budget in
which she adds 20 percent to the 40 percent that her
boss has already added, because she knows the record
company will automatically subtract 20 percent on top

of the 20 percent they subtracted from the budget they already cut in half.

14. The record company officially hires the director! Everyone agrees that they have made the right choice, especially the director. Then the production company adds 10 percent to the budget because they know they can now. Then the record company subtracts 20 percent to show who's boss. Then the production company adds back 5 percent, and then the record company subtracts 3 percent.

15. Everybody threatens to quit.

16. Everybody decides to come back because the job is booked! By now, everybody is so confused that they think they're getting a good deal.

17. Everybody agrees that they're all really talented, unlike everybody else.

18. The record company swears that this is the most money they've ever paid for a video, but that this one really deserves it.

19. The production company swears that they will not even ask for a single, solitary overage. This policy holds true until the first day of shooting, when the whole process starts all over again.

17

RIP in Heaven

So, I take it we are all agreed that it was a malfunction of the O-ring (which was adjacent to the b/c outflow) that provoked the 'incident,' leading to the one hundred thousand gallons of water that leaked, flooded, and ultimately reduced to rubble two commercial soundstages, plus all the equipment, plus the three Toyota RAV sports utility vehicles lying therein?" asks James B. Clerk, the world's most renowned authority on ridiculous water gizmos.

"Uh, I think I speak for all of us," I begin tentatively, "when I say that whatever you just said, we all totally agree with you."

Three nail-biting special effects technicians, two sweating commercial insurance reviewers, four tight-assed liability lawyers, and the creepiest of all my badly dressed company accountants all nod sagely. Like they know a b/c outflow from a hair on their balls.

"But what we *really* want to know is," I continue, "does that mean that *my* insurance company owes me eight hundred and fifty thousand dollars, or what?"

"Well," he replies slowly, "that would all come down to this one, single, solitary question . . ."

Mr. Clerk, who's the only guy on earth who knows about O-rings and outflows, thanks to his cutting-edge engineering work on several Las Vegas hotel water fountains that can squirt in perfect syncopated rhythm to Vivaldi's *Four Seasons*, waves his arms to indicate the behemoth conference table, which is piled sky-high with diagrams, charts, and photographic re-creations that have been studied, dissected, and meticulously scrutinized a thousand times. We all lean in and bite our tongues as if he was about to reveal the exact latitude and longitude of the real location of the official holy grail.

"Was the aforementioned O-ring (which was adjacent to the b/c outflow water valve) lined with double-coated ninety-percent rayon thin-weave brush? *Or* was it covered in untreated one-hundred-percent Australian horsehair?"

I stare in horror at Sam, the owner of the special effects company, who is seated directly across from me, hemming, hawing, and gently hyperventilating in a desperate effort to stall for time. Because if he answers this question *incorrectly*, then *my* insurance company will refuse *my* claim, and I will have to sue *his* pathetic, uninsured ass for it, which will take us decades and cost us millions, and he'll be ruined, and I'll be ruined.

"Um, I was just wondering," I interrupt. "Which one means the insurance company pays?"

I bat my eyelashes in a saucy, cartoonesque fashion in the dim hopes that the Vegas water man will feel that I like him, so he'll feel that he likes me, so he'll just tell the insurance company to pay me a million bucks and let us all go home. Because I *really, really, really* need the $850,000 that I lost five and a half weeks ago when I allowed the snotty French director to purchase a special-effects upside-down-waterfall machine, so that he could drive the truck he was making a commercial for through it *right side up*, which just makes the truck look upside down again anyway. The upside-down-waterfall machine blew itself up and flooded two production soundstages, a few Toyota trucks, and all the props, lighting, and grip equipment, not to mention the plush Italian leather clutch that I got on sale at Barneys last month, which still cost me $500 anyway.

Oh God, I really liked that purse.

Meanwhile, with his eyes closed and his fists balled and his jaw clenched tighter than a duck's vagina, Special-Effects Sam takes a moment to collect his thoughts before he opens his mouth. Because it's my guess that Sam has no idea what an O-ring is, let alone what it was lined with, because he is now so stressed out that he's fallen off his wagon and has gotten stoned on so much pot, vodka, and cough syrup that he can't even remember why he got so stressed out and fell off the wagon in the first place. I pray to God, Allah, and Buddha to guide him correctly.

Then Sam takes his best shot.

"Uhhhhhhhhh . . . horsehair?"

All eyes swivel toward James B. Clerk.

He nods just as sagely as we all nodded when we didn't know what the fuck *he* was talking about.

"Just as I thought!" he says confidently. "Your design was correct! So this incident is what we refer to as 'mechanical error,' or 'an act of God,' and is therefore covered under the conditions of the O Pictures policy."

Oh thank you, acts of all gods, even the crazy robot dieties of that naughty L. Ron Hubbard, whose minions tried to convert my three-year-old son at the Orange Grove Dianetics Nursery School back in 1975, when I thought Scientology had something to do with magnets. The insurance company pays! My company will not go broke! I will not be made bankrupt! My personal home will not seized by federal authorities in order to pay the taxes on losing almost a million dollars so that a silly European could create a shitty advertisement for an ugly gas-guzzling SUV!

Under normal circumstances, I would take just a few moments to consider my charmed ride before getting right back on the trouble train. Because once again, I have bucked the odds and lived to fight another day, just like on the Mr. Mister video, when we had our tires shot out on the Hollywood Freeway and $11,000 in petty cash got hijacked by Mexican drug runners and we figured out a way to charge it to the record company as a craft service overage. Or like on the R.E.M. video, when we burned down the last functioning soundstage on the island of Manhattan right after I got shot at in a coffee shop on the Lower East Side trying to order a bagel at four in the morning and the insurance company blamed it all on the porn film shooting on the third floor. Or like on the Taco Bell commercial, when I dropped $5,000 on blackjack at the express order of a coked-up advertising agency producer right before I went into the Puerto Rican jungle with four different neurotoxic insect repellents sprayed on every inch of my body and emerged six hours later with asthma, severe chafing, and 649 mosquito bites on (just) my lower torso, and got a free, 100 percent comped vacation for my entire family to the beautiful island of St. Lucia!

What has become increasingly obvious is that horrible stuff keeps happening to me because I keep doing horrible stuff. Twenty years ago, I wanted to participate in great works of art. Then I settled for making big piles of money instead. Now I'm just trying to keep from being eaten alive.

But this time, things are going to be different. Because this time I've pledged a solemn vow: if the Creator(ess) of the universe allows me to beat the rap on the horsehair O-ring, I have solemnly sworn to quit my job, go out of business, and never produce another rock video or commercial ever, ever again.

Why?

For fifteen years, O Pictures has stalked me. Wherever I went, it went, and whatever I did, it did, salivating at my heels, just like Señor Señor, my second ex-boyfriend's mother's third Chihuahua rescue, who spent his declining years shredding my Achilles tendons until somebody left the front door open and he got run over by a speeding Webber's bread truck.

Hallelujah. Just like a little dog under a big semi, O Pictures would now be pulped. For the first time in my life, I had the money, time, and inclination to do nothing, and for the first time in my life, it sounded pretty good to me.

I thought about selling it, loaning it, merging it, or renting it out. But in the end, O Pictures was only me, and I was done. Bye-bye.

I let go of my employees, said goodbye to my accountant, boxed up the files, sent back the copiers, ripped down the curtains, pulled up the carpets, sold the filing cabinets, donated the office supplies, cleared the computers, turned off the lights, walked out, went home, and fucked my husband for the first time in one and a half decades without worrying about a stupid fruit plate.

Free at last, lord.

Oh God, I was so happy.

Oh shit, I was so bored.

Because, guess what? I didn't have a job anymore.

Of course, I didn't *want* a job anymore, but that's beside the point. For years I had lived simply, from crisis to crisis. As a top-tier executive of my very own company, I had always been way too busy delegating demeaning tasks to others to do any of them myself. How was I supposed to know where to buy Tampax, or how to grill salmon, or when to change lightbulbs, or how to flea-dip the cat? That's what all those psycho personal assistants got paid for—when they weren't too busy shooting smack or stealing my toilet paper, that is.

In the meantime, I had no idea how to structure a day without deluge.

Some people thrive on protein, and some people live on love, but I counted on *conflict* to giveth and then taketh away. Conflict created turmoil, turmoil induced stress, stress promoted adrenaline, and adrenaline produced energy, so I could continue the conflict, so I could stay up all night, so I could start getting worked up for a new conflict all over again.

Producing had not been my job, it had been my *mission*. All day, all night, all my soul for MTV. If I could squeeze that pop star into a size-four leotard by six, I could save the world! If she couldn't rumba by eight, the polar ice caps would melt. Every muddle justified my vigilance. Every mop-up confirmed my duty. I had been anointed—it was my duty to implement peace and posterity by bringing pop to the people.

The point had been to stay so busy that I wouldn't have to think about what made me want to stay so busy. Now, the luxury of a numbed mind was as hard to get a hold of as a Jackson's nose bone.

After my job, all that was left of me was—well—*me*. This implied that I would no longer be able to camouflage my flawed personal character by robing it in a professional alias. For years I had been making friends and influencing people solely on the basis of my job description:

"Hi. Who are you?"

"I'm Sharon Oreck. I'm a rock video producer!"

"Oh. What are rock videos?"

"Rock videos are what I produce!"

"Really. Well, what do rock video producers do?"

"They produce rock videos!"

"Okay, when you produce, what do you do?"

"I do rock videos!"

"Do you have any ideas, opinions, or personal anecdotes?"

"No! Did I mention that I'm a rock video producer?"

With the loss of my one-stop doppelgänger, I would now be forced to negotiate my way through the world with good manners, human decency, or cold cash. Worse, I might be tempted to trot out my long-suppressed real personality, a thing which my own best friend, Margaret Goldsmith, had advised me to administer with extreme caution during a moment of unusual candor in November 1979, after spending seven days and nights with the largest and last shipment of prerevolutionary Iranian opium ever to arrive in America.

"Um, I don't think we don't have boyfriends because we're too fat," Margaret posited while sprawled delicately on the dining room table in a pink bath mat and matching turban that nicely complemented her red-rimmed eyes. "I think we just have bad personalities. Like, I'm kinda wishy-washy, and you're sort of a bitch."

She was right. Without my O, I was a naked, crabby thing. Sure, I had shed some baggage, but with it had gone my mantle—the blanket of power, coolness, and entitlement that I had woven to protect me from pedigree, talent, or virtue. Now I had no idea what was going to happen next. At least when I was working, I could be sure it was going to be something bad.

"Oh, Dr. Brinker . . ." I whined to my Dutch postcognitive psychotherapist during our last session in her Beverly Hills office, which was conveniently located right next door to the Rodeo Drive shopping district. "Why am I so totally psycho?"

I was depressed because I'd just spent $500 in the Barneys perfumed-soap department, and they hadn't even paid for my parking.

"You are so fucking psycho because you are so fucking smart!" Hannah responded automatically. After all, unlike my leg waxer, I didn't pay Hannah two hundred bucks an hour to tell me how attractive I was.

"You would be fucking stupid not to be fucking psycho in a crazy place like this!"

I was suddenly flooded with insight. Maybe my peer group was a bad influence. Maybe they were all nutjobs, and I was not. Maybe I had just caught a depressive narcissistic personality disorder that I could get rid of, if I were only around *normal* people.

"Okay, maybe I'll go someplace else. Maybe I'll be happy if I'm in a happier place."

"Fuck that fuckermother place if it doesn't work out!"

It was Hannah's unique therapeutic approach to employ stentorian, filth-laced invective to blame everyone in the entire world except me for everything that had ever happened to me. If you ask me, this is one of the few things in life worth paying for. Sadly, despite a master's degree from the Amsterdam Pot-Smoking Hippie Psychology University, Hannah had not mastered the nuances of modern American expletives.

I began the beginning of the rest of my life by going to Australia, where my husband was shooting *The Matrix* for a year. What a fantastic country, if you don't count the restaurant service; the butt worms; the tiny jellyfish that can penetrate your wet suit so they can paralyze your lungs with a single agonizing sting; the big red spiders that nest in your shoes so they can sink their venomous pincers into your flesh so they can cause total respiratory collapse; and the really adorable monotreme pseudomammals, who have duck beaks and monkey heads and deadly poisonous tail spurs that melt your major organs. For some reason, everything that is cute everywhere else is fatal in Australia.

Okay, I learned how to ride a horse.

I started doing yoga. I started to write.

I came home. I quit riding a horse. I started a different kind of yoga.

I moved.

A Hispanic man of medium height wearing a brown plaid shirt invaded my house when I was all alone and chased me down the stairs. I screamed so loud that a Disney executive who lived two canyons over jumped in his car to rescue me.

I walked around with a baseball bat for four weeks. Then I didn't get my period, so I thought I was pregnant. My doctor said I was just stressed out, so did I want:

1. A synthetic progesterone pill or
2. A natural progesterone shot?

I said, "Natural, of course," and the nurse promptly gave me an injection that was the size of my head. Then my butt really started hurting, and it got really red, and it kept getting worse, until it looked like I was cooking a carton of Ostrich eggs in there. I am the only person in the history of Queen of Angels Good Samaritan Hospital who has ever had a butt scan.

Finally, I got put in the hospital with a potential case of necrotizing strep in my ass, and at least one million medical students came in to inspect my hindquarters. It was a very unusual case.

I recovered, and then our new house flooded, and we had to sue the people we had bought it from, and it cost thousands and thousands and took years and years, and then the case finally went to arbitration, where we accepted a rather high offer after the judge began to refer to the defendants as "the liars."

Then I met the little red head of my first grandchild, Harper.

Then I met the little red head of my second grandchild, Tess.

Then I met the little brown head of my third grandchild, William.

My mom and dad are healthy and wealthy, and they live in a big house in the Palisades.

My mom goes to Tuscany every year to pick out a ton of carrera marble, which she has shipped to her Westside studio, so she can sculpt gigantic Jewish-themed objets d'art. She has a ten-foot mezuzah right next to the front door. I'm not kidding.

My dad is still selling fine discount office furniture. For some inexplicable reason, he collects hotel keys and artificial apples. My dad's best friend of fifty-two years, Stan Apollo, still comes over every other Wednesday to play poker.

My sister moved to a kibbutz and got married to an ex-Englishman. Then he inherited a million dollars, so they abandoned their socialist principles and moved to a big new house in a suburb near Tel Aviv. I have two nieces who are cuter than pie. One just graduated from junior high and the other one graduated from art school in Chicago and lives in Tel Aviv.

Mary lives around the corner and is still in the movie business. In fact, we made a documentary about the fourteen women in the 2004 U.S. Senate. It is called, duh, *14 Women*.

I'm still married to Bill Pope, and he's still so fucking hot, you wouldn't believe it. If you are either of my children, I am sorry you had to read that.

My son, Josh, is a grown man, and he is very handsome and smart, and an accomplished and successful documentary filmmaker. I don't want to say that he is perfect, but I can't help it, because I am a big Jew. He's never ever done anything wrong, except once, back in the nineties, when he refused to get out of show business and become an architect. Now he has one perfect wife and three perfect children and one really cool house. I promised Harper that I would mention how much I love her. Here's how much: a scadillion billion grillion.

My daughter is nineteen and a student at Middlebury College. She won the Ben and Jerry's Environmental Action Lick Global Warming Contest. She came up with a plan to convert her Vermont boarding school to wind power, raised the money to furnish it with a wind turbine, and won a year's supply of ice cream for her idea. Just in case she wants to know, I prefer Fudge Chunk and Bananas on the Rum.

My ex-partner runs his own company and is happy and successful. Whenever I see him, he's really nice to me. Why couldn't he be that way before?

Herb died. I never saw him again.

Larry died. I never saw him again.

I know people who are sick or were sick or will get sick, and some of them I will never see again.

There are dead grips, and dead gaffers, and dead singers, and dead VCR dudes whose names I never knew or could never remember, and I never saw them again.

Sometimes I see people I worked with and they remember me, and things I said, and things I did, and they don't remember that they made me cry. They tell me that they loved me, and respected me, and admired me, and that those times together were so, so special.

Are you fucking crazy, I think. Don't you remember?

Then it comes back. The crosses burning, the mirrors dissolving, the rowboat in the fog, the boys leaping, the girls twirling in muslin, my friends, my employees, my dirty, filthy coworkers cleaving to one another in the cold, brutal dawns. I see Herb's glasses glinting in the Malibu sun, and the mermen leaping behind him and Madonna playing in the water.

They stay with me, after the rage, after the anguish, the money spent, the privilege, the popularity long behind.

Oh God, it was fun.

Oh God, I miss it.

Thank God it's over.

Acknowledgments

I started writing *Video Slut*, by accident, in 1999 while intention-
ally attending Kathy Kohlman's uber-creative writing class, where
I attempted not to vomit on a weekly basis owing to the stress of
having to read my assignments out loud to my uber-creative
classmates, who included an actual rocket scientist, an award-
winning screenwriter, a hunky sword-and-sandal enthusiast, and
a super-glamorous diamond-encrusted billionaire divorcé who
apologized to us on the last day of class for being (inappropri-
ately) aggressive while being (totally) drunk during all of our
writing critique sessions. Kathy is a great friend and mentor, and
I owe her. Big Time. Millions of thanks to Phil Joanou, who told
me about her.

I would also like to formally thank and issue great big gobs
of eternal love and gratitude to Robin Sue Sloane Seibert, Alisa
Tager, Becky Johnston, Sara Melson, Nancy Rommelman, and
Ann Biderman, who read (all) my stuff and told me what to fix
and how to fix it and suggested that I might try to stop being a big
fat baby and finish the frickin' thing already. Also, Ann codified
the term "Video Slut." It's so good.

To Linda Lichter, my adorable-est lawyer and beloved pal,
thank you, thank you, thank you for everything, not least of all
introducing me to my Super Agent (and living god), David Kuhn,

who makes all things possible. Hats off to Billy Kingsland for being awesome enough to know that the truck in the "Material Girl" video was brown, not black.

At Faber and Faber, I have been lucky beyond belief to have had two editors who believed in me. First Denise Oswald, who bought my book, and made me laugh and really made me feel good about myself, because she's the coolest girl in the world. She also freely shared her limitless wisdom and patience and some really good gossip about deceased authors and rock stars. Now I have Mitzi (my) Angel, who has gently and lovingly nudged me to actually finish this book and is one of the best things that ever happened to me. I heart her. I also way-heart Chantal Clarke, who always looks after me and is my Facebook friend.

Meanwhile, although I would of course like to thank all of the sexual partners who contributed to the "Slut" part of this memoir, the "Video" part is indebted to the people and artists (okay, they're people too) whom I worked with from 1984 to 1999. To all the people at Limelight, including Steve, Tim, Fay, Howard, Crystal, Tracette, Ann, and wonderful, hilarious Simon, thanks for just being cool enough to be there. To Mary Lambert, who was my first significant partner in (video) crime, and who always stuck with me and who still believes in me, even when I make her really nervous by exposing her in a brutally snarky way in my personal memoirs, I love you.

At NO Pics, I began working with many people whom I continued to work with for the rest of my producing life, with the exception of the Partner, who is still quite frankly the handsomest, grooviest, video-est guy in town. I am in awe that he continues to grow and prosper, especially since I was already exhausted a decade or two ago. Pardon my (former) youth, Partner. It is always a pleasure to see you.

To Dustin Robertson, thank you for your lifetime of O Pictures love.

To Jo Ann Thraillkill, Lisa Levine, Alexa Balatsos, Kate Miller, Lynn Risden Rush(!), Al, Paula, Maria, Alison, plus all the weird accountants, crazy personal assistants, and Margarita, who cleaned up the mess, I love you (more).

To Michael Patterson, Candace Reckinger, Oley Sassone, Lyndall Hobbs, Geoffrey Edwards, Kevin Kerslake, Matthew Rolston, Herb Ritts, Kim Dempster, Phil Joanou, Eric Ifergan, Noah Bogen, Eric Goode, Serge Becker, Geoff Moore, Ellen Von Unwerth, Evan Bernard, Pam Thomas, Peggy Sirota, Geoff Barrish, and Bronwen Hughes, thanks for the (incredible) memories.

To Anita, XXOO times eternity.

To Matt Mahurin, who taught me the meaning of genius, I love you. Thanks for the cover. And everything else . . .

To Tamra, Kim, and Tom Davis, thanks for letting me be your other family. XX.

To Savannah, who is proud to be the daughter of a Video Slut, I love you. Way more.

To the Orecks who made me, and the Orecks whom I made, I love you (dedication).

To the Israels, ditto.

And then there is Bill Pope, the love of my life and the life of my love. As Autograph put it so succinctly, you are a real fuckin' fucker.